Dreams of a Woman

Dreams of a Woman
An Analyst's Inner Journey

Sheila Moon

Sigo Press
Boston

SIGO PRESS
77 North Washington Street, 201
Boston, Massachusetts 02114

Publisher and General Editor: Sisa Sternback-Scott
Associate Editor: Becky Goodman

ISBN 0–938434–17–9   ISBN 0–938434–14–4
Library of Congress Cataloging in Publication Data

Moon, Sheila.
    Dreams of a woman.

    1. Moon, Sheila.   2. Psychoanalysts—Biography.
3. Dreams.   I. Title.
RC339.52.M63A33   1983   616.89'092'4 [B]   83–10826
ISBN 0–938434–17–9
ISBN 0–938434–14–4(pbk.)

Cover Illustration: Kevin Gaines
Set in ITC Garamond.
Printed in the United States of America.

Table of Contents

List of Illustrations

Foreword

Writing a Foreword to an autobiographical book is a difficult task. I do so in this instance because the plan of this book arose from my many discussions with the author. Also I feel a debt of gratitude to her for having been allowed to share her experience.

This book is an unusual account of an individuation process which has been worked with by the author for nearly fifty years. She deals with the joys, sorrows, difficulties, rewards with a rare sense of honesty, of modesty, with no sense of inflation. In this autobiography the author gives a rich account of the continuity of her inner life, and also clarifies and illumines this picture with psychological knowledge and religious wisdom. Through the whole work one feels the deep search for an understanding of the extreme opposites in her nature which were rooted in traumatic events of her ancestral past.

The effects of these traumatic events became manifest in her early youth. At that time her search for spiritual values was fiercely shaken by a terrifying dream of cosmic proportions, in which she felt herself condemned to live under the power of the Devil. For a long time she was filled with fear and a feeling of guilt for the darkness of life and the darkness of the world. Insofar as this dream was awakening her to consciousness, it became the grace of her life as well as a curse.

One rarely participates in such a deep process of self-realization poised continuously on the edge of life and death. Those who read this will be moved, as I myself was, by the intensity of the fight with the evil powers in the unconscious, with the dark spirit of the soul, as well as by the continual courageous attempts to overcome the frightening tension between Light and Darkness. The unique help given to the writer through all the years came from the exceptional brightness of her mind and the exceptional religious instinct she possessed. This capacity for spiritual awareness, her high degree of inner integrity, and her sense of religious-psychological values proved to be inestimable gifts in her struggle with life.

Thus she became "victorious" in an absolute and rich way. As a highly gifted woman, she found it not at all easy to sacrifice slowly her intellectual powers. That is to say, she had to submit to the higher authority in her soul and to establish a relation to her inner center. Through such suffering she came to the realization that "the relation of the individual spirit to the God Presence was central from the first."

I shall not comment on the various phases of her rich life. Their discovery comes with the reading of the book. However, I would draw attention to a few inner episodes. Among the many important inner experiences she had, was an "initiation" into the mysteries of an American Indian tribe. There she got in touch with the profound spirit of nature to counterbalance the Logos aspect of her mind. Thus, instead of falling again into the trap of the threatening negative inner animus, she had the insight that she herself was a feminine being, that she was "woman and earth." She became aware of her repressed feeling capacities, of the nobility of her love, her compassion and sympathy for all suffering creatures, human or lower animal.

A further significant realization was the recognition that she herself as a being was important. She discovered her own unique reality which she understood as a constant becoming a part of the Other which is larger than the personal Self. At the end of this book she comes in touch with her own deep creativity and with the transcendent supra-personal forces of the psyche. This process was a part of her acceptance of her own Demon who had "driven my being over and over with a deadly fire." Now she was prepared to say the words of a new creation, "I am." With this insight she could accept the deep mystery overshadowing her life.

In spite of (and of course because of) these experiences, Sheila Moon always retains her feeling for the human being, and has throughout a refreshing sense of humor.

I believe that readers will find in this autobiographical work much help, much illumination, and much encouragement for undertaking their own Quest of the Self.

Dr. Liliane Frey-Rohn
Zurich, Switzerland

Preface

This morning (of all days, my brother's birthday) I reread all of my earliest "inner" accounts of ME (or perhaps, accounts of inner ME) and realized that, in some way this is precisely where the beginning must be even if there is no end. I must risk myself thus, by describing myself from the viewpoint of all the least "academic" and least "scientific" methods—which proved to be so very very accurate! When I opened up to these analyses of me, made in 1940, 1942, 1955, and 1956 (graphological, chirological, numerological, astrological), each one done with no knowledge of the other, it was so startling and so explosive that I had to write poems all day just to keep myself in hand. I, who scorned "unscientific" methods, had had each of these "things" done for me by people reputable and trustworthy. They did not know each other at the time, nor did any of them know me before they did the analyses. Yet each of them set forth on a broad canvas the painting of my life—painting the same subject from different angles—that subject I knew almost nothing about (in depth, consciously) until I was almost thirty.

Before that, all I can remember of any conscious consideration of my "inside self," was when a close friend of mine took me to see a very strange and wonderful old woman who did horoscopes. She refused to do mine because she said that it was too difficult for me to encompass at that time. I think I let it pass with very little conscious affect. What would have happened differently had she done it, I cannot know. And when I was eighteen or nineteen, I had a Terrible Dream of cosmic proportions. I did not understand anything about that, either. Except in this case it affected me deeply, no matter how I tried to forget it, and I sweated out a depression with no help because I knew of none. And did not know how to talk about it without being thought insane.

From 1940 until now I have worked at my inner psychological-religious journey. Because it has been so long, so overflowing with destruction and creation, loss and gain, death and life, it seems that perhaps I owe a debt to Life (and to Kazantzakis' *Cry of God*) to try to trace my journeyings in such a way as to encourage others that it is in fact worthwhile to try to know one's Self. That it can in fact be approximated. That perhaps the deepest gift that can be given by men to this suffering universe is to stammer my goings and comings.

I have no intention of writing pages of lurid (or dull) memoirs. I am not writing an autobiography in any usual sense. I am going to try to trace and describe the voyage of one small but singular ship across the vast reaches of inner space, describing in part where it went, the times it almost foundered in storms or went aground on rocks or was boarded by enemies, the times it put in to sheltering bays, found supplies in unexpected places, and how its crew fared during these long years. (The Ancient Mariner indeed it feels to have as captain!)

It is not possible to do this! Everything in me resists it except my self who keeps saying, "Go on! Do it!" But how? And how to avoid inflation, self-denigration, dishonesty, banality, and all other dreadful attitudes which can accompany self-revelation? Not other-revelation, for that is one thing I will not do. But how to make self-revelation non-egocentric, make it helpful in a genuine way to others, make it "true" in the deepest sense possible? These are my questions as I face the opening of doors, questions to which I am certain I will not have answers until this Thing is finished—or is at least well begun.

Emily Dickinson said, in one of her poems, "Not knowing when the dawn will come/ I open every door;/ Or has it feathers like a bird,/ Or billows like a shore?"

But how is it honest—even possible—to say "I open every door"? Even if Emily said so. Meant it. To a remarkable degree, did so. Any life is incredibly mysterious, complex, beyond all explanations. It happens nonetheless, moves inexorably from its beginning to its end, and we each have the choice between entering into our humanity as religiously intentional beings, or being pushed and pulled along by currents we don't try to understand, eventually to be beached and, crying for our natural element, to perish.

Perhaps to try to open every door is at least to pay homage to whatever a life is when its tenant has tried to inhabit this dwelling as consciously as possible for the duration permitted. I'm certain that I've not been to that degree and thus far as responsible and honest a tenant of my life as Emily was of hers. I am convinced of her peerlessness! I am also convinced—now, and after much doubt—that to try to open every door of my life's journey is my gift to my planetary sisters and brothers who are working along with me for a greater comprehension of what their being here amounts to.

So it is one voyage "where no end is"—mine—that will be chronicled as a hopefully relevant sort of a paradigm for others.

S.M.

Dreams of a Woman

Where is my dwelling place?
    Where stands nor I nor Thou.
Where is my final end,
    to which I needs must go?

It is where no end is.
    Then whither shall I press?
On even beyond God,
    into a wilderness.

Angelus Silesius

I

Open Every Door (through 1940)

The first ten years of my life were good ones. I came with Halley's comet, which wasn't a bad beginning. But the first World War arrived before I was in kindergarten, and left its mark on those years probably more than I can know. I do remember the first Armistice Day, and driving in our old touring car around and around the town square. I know I was a bright child with a high IQ, and I went to kindergarten at the University of Utah's special school for such bright kids. My early memories are centered on the various creatures that I collected alive, and loved, and watched. Also I know I read early. And, so my mother said, refused ever to talk baby talk.

Because I was born on Christmas Day, and my parents were married on Hallowe'en, holidays were festive. We went to the mountains during the summer, either to a small house we rented or to a fishing resort. I remember watching the wild creatures—

squirrels, birds, lizards, chipmunks, marmots and playing in a creek or at the edge of a lake. I also loved music, as it came to me on our old hand-wound Victrola or on the piano.

My mother had lost her first child, a girl, and so I suffered from her overprotection and anxiety in my earlier years. When my brother came—I was three—he seemed to get the attention, partly because he was sickly as a little child. I felt caught between things I didn't understand. You were fussed over too much, or you were not heard when you wanted to be fussed over. But on the whole our lives were good and the usual middle middle-class. My parents seemed to be almost magical at times. They loved to ballroom dance and won prizes doing it. I can still remember lying on their bed while they got ready to go to a dance—my mother in a black gown with spangles on it, my father in a tuxedo. They seemed like characters from a fairytale then, and I adored them.

The kindergarten and early school years were not bad for me, but then all sorts of changes came rushing together and getting all tangled up. We left the Rocky Mountain region and came to California. I am not sure why we did. Somehow it seemed, in a hidden way, not told to me, it had to do with my father's changing his job when he should not have done so. It remains a mystery. It is of course only one thread in the tangle. But it meant moving, and leaving behind friends, school, and the familiar things. It meant another kind of landscape and climate. More than all else it meant that I moved from childhood to puberty. Being in the upper percentiles with regard to intelligence is one thing— and it has benefits as well as drawbacks. Being in the lower percentiles with regard to appearance is quite another. That is where I was. I was shy, with few social graces: if you add to that a terrible acne you have a disaster. For me, it was. I wanted to hide, to cover myself with something, to keep away from peers. My mother was attractive in a gypsy sort of way. Any boys I brought home gravitated to her. She laughed easily and liked gaiety. I did not laugh easily then, and there was no way I could be joyful when strangers stopped me on the street to tell me about a cure for acne.

Entering the high school years was a torment. I was younger than most of my classmates. I was, from my viewpoint, uglier than any of them. Being Christian Scientists, my family did little to tackle the problem of acne. For awhile I had ultraviolet light treatments which did not help. The boys drawn to me were in the same condition I was. So I carried my heart well guarded, and I loosed my mind, which was a good steel and ready to use.

One of the saddest things about people creatures is that we can do this. We can put part of ourselves into a cement cell-block for life (unless sometime we find an inner lawyer for the defense), and we can then lead our existence by caring for our strengths alone. If this imprisonment is done with the skill with which I did it, then we suffer, I suspect, for the rest of our lives trying to break the defenses. It is not enough to see that we have them. It is more like, having learned that under that abandoned castle of stone on the plain there is a treasure, we learn at the same time that there is no way to tear the castle down except with our bare hands. Long and painful work—if indeed it can be accomplished. The bloody-handed removal of each resistant stone is a prayer and, if fortunate, we may make an opening even into the subbasement before we die. Those who follow may get totally through and find much more treasure, reason enough for working so hard.

Before adolescence had attacked me with its troubles, there was in me always—as far back as I can remember—not only a love for books and music, but a love for fantasy. I lived in the generation of *St. Nicholas Magazine,* the Oz books, *Wind in the Willows,* the Pooh chronicles. My own imagination was racing much of the time in childhood. This trait has continued as a great river taking me on many journeys, evil ones and good ones, joyful ones and sad ones, but it has never cast me ashore. It stands behind my poetry, behind my novels, and behind my love for the writings about myths and folktales.

My first overwhelming "falling in love" came in here, also. A boy actually gave me his high school ring, and then took it back in a scene I can still feel, though I can't remember why. A few times I tried to charm some boy or other but it never worked out.

Finally I stopped trying and became an achiever.

I was in the high school honor society, graduated at the age of seventeen and went on immediately to the university. One year later when the depression struck my family, I left school and went to work—in a factory, in an office at a switchboard, in a dinky office of a dinky weekly newspaper, and finally in some of the university offices so that I could take more courses. These were turbulent years of work, fatigue, weekends of drinking and letdowns. Some poetry got written—rather awful poetry, as I look at it now—but it helped to keep me from totally foundering. I had moved away from home, so my life was spent either at a dull job or with friends in like circumstances.

Nonetheless, in the midst of all the depression disasters I did begin to study in night school, for university credit, choosing premedical studies, as I wanted to be a brain surgeon. Except for some good times with family and friends, hiking, swimming, loafing, by and large, it was work hard during the week and roister hard over the weekend.

It was somewhere in here that I had the Terrible Dream.

(0)

I am with two friends on the top of a very high building—one in the process of construction, so that only the heavy iron frame, with many floors, is finished. Otherwise the entire structure is open to the elements. One friend suddenly slips and starts to fall over the edge. Terrified, I reach out instantly and grasp her hand with one of mine. With my other hand I grasp the hand of the other friend, as if to save us. But all three of us are falling through space toward the ground, from the top of this building. When I land, the others have disappeared. I lie alone on the street. A huge truck comes along and runs over my body. Then I know I am dead. I get up and begin wandering through the streets of a city, a medieval city (although I had not yet been in one). There are cobbled streets and strange dark buildings. I come into a large square (European). In its center is a table with places set and food on it. People come and sit at the table. I join them. Near me is Fred (a red-headed and very hot-headed man I knew, who was later killed in an automobile accident). I lean toward him and say, "I'm dead and in hell and I belong to the devil." He laughs. I ask him angrily if he has any matches. He nods and pulls from his pocket a handful of kitchen matches. I breathe on them. They burst into flames. Everyone at the table flees and I am left utterly alone in a deserted square in a deserted city.

I awoke in terror, and after finally falling asleep again, dreamed:

I am in bed, in a cell-like room on an upper floor. It is night. Suddenly I realize that a man wearing a black cape (or wings) is standing on my windowsill. Half afraid and half magnetized, I arise in my nightgown and step onto the windowsill. He stretches out his caped arms (or wings) and folds them around me. Together we step out into the nothingness of the night sky, flying above the earth.

As far as I can recall, I didn't write the Terrible Dream down at that time. I was much too terrified and bewildered and eager to forget it. But such vivid images needed no further record. I knew nothing about an inner life then nor did I have religious resources. As I mentioned, my family had been Christian Scientists and I attended the Sunday School programs because of this. However, it had been easy for me to sever all my connections with the Church when I had been exposed directly to the narrowness and judgmentalism of the church through the attitudes of its officers.

At about the age of fourteen, when I then attended church regularly, a friend from a neighboring town and I had gotten a marvelous book on sex. She brought it and lent it to me and we were having a wonderful time going through it and finding out things that we didn't know. At that time, I played the organ in the church Sunday school. My friend and I would usually meet on Sundays because she lived so far away. One Sunday when I was to return the book to my friend, I brought this book to church. But I made this mistake, actually I don't think it was a mistake, it was a cosmic nudge. I left the book on the organ bench. At the end of the class, the superintendent who was a sourpuss anyway, stood up and said, "Someone in this group has a book that they should not have, I trust they will come up and speak to me at the end of the Sunday school." So I walked up at the end of the church school, took the book and walked out and I have never been in a Christian Science Church since that time.

After the Terrible Dream I plunged into an anxious depression of huge, almost overwhelming proportions. The outer Depression also added to the situation. It was a grim time. I went to work because I had to eat. I ate because I had to work. When I could I drank to forget. My friends couldn't understand what was happening because I knew I couldn't tell them. They rather disapproved of my existence already. Somewhere in here a strange coincidence brought into the circle of those I knew a young man, working and studying to be a chiropractor. We became very close. Through him I met an Anglican priest whose name was Father Hill. I was baptized and confirmed in the church where my friend was a member, often helping to serve mass. I became the organist there. Father Hill was a gentle, loving insightful man. He got hold of me at this very youthful time when I had few resources and was at a very low, depressed place. He brought me to a new place—I wouldn't say a place of peace but a place where slowly the depression lifted and I walked on more solid ground. With work, a new religious undergirding, and a fast-paced hedonism, I think I forced the dream from my awareness as much as it was possible to do.

Seven or eight years came between my meeting the priest and the right time to open the first door into my darkness. I was still working days, but now in the university offices. I had moved nearer the campus, sharing an apartment with one of the friends in the Terrible Dream. I studied, worked, smoked, drank, swam, studied, sometimes rested.

For the time being I went on in the office and in the classroom, finishing my premedical work with a major in psychology (this was nearest to being a brain surgeon, I suppose), a double minor in philosophy and English, and, by the skin of my teeth, Phi Beta Kappa.

The only psychology course that I had not had was one I did not want. I took it for convenience. I did not make a choice, really, and yet something did make a choice. The professor, a woman, pushed aside the academic attitudes and led us into the depth psychologies of Dr. Fritz Kunkel and Dr. Carl Jung. I had not heard of either of them before, the university department of psychology being very behavioristic. The professor and I soon became friends. She introduced me to the possibility that there was such a thing as a psychological-religious journey (as both Kunkel and Jung had talked about) and that it was available to me.

Through this professor I eventually met a friend of hers who led summer seminars in a combination of material from the synoptic Gospels and the psychology of Dr. Kunkel. At last I was beginning to find that somewhere people were talking about their inner selves and their inner meanings! I grew increasingly interested in the matters of being and Being. I learned that others had experiences like my Terrible Dream, and depressions. I could talk about them.

Shortly before graduation, I met a Dutch lawyer who fell deeply in love with me. Although I was then too emotionally immature to reciprocate much, he was very important and our relationship deepened, lasting until his death almost twenty-five years later. My "graduation" was from one life to another, so startling were these new doors.

The Terrible Dream was for some time an entrance blocked. The first revelation of possibilities of meaning in my selfness, in a possible self-world dialog was both an exit from a destructive prison and an open door into Life. My spiritual longings could be explored. My artist side could be acceptable. My anxieties could be shared as belonging to humanity. At last I plunged, and began Jungian analysis.

One of the first requests from my analyst was that I have my handwriting analyzed by a well-known graphologist, Max Zeller, a recent refugee from Nazi Germany. Very skeptical, I sent a sample of my handwriting to him.

I am leaving for 6 Europe — including Zurich (in Zu this month — could you please to give me answers to the following

I quote verbatim some of the comments this then-unknown man made about me. (I met him personally later, and came to know him and his family as friends. He was one of the warmest and most genuine people I have known. He died in 1978.)

> . . . [B]oth her strength and weakness result from her matter-of factness . . . has almost completely eliminated the subjective factor . . . no passion . . . [P]atience, justice, ability to watch and concentrate, make her an excellent research worker . . . excellent intellect . . . lovingly cautious . . . good adaptability, objectivity . . . can feel with others . . . but in great conflict . . . does not satisfy that tendency in her that is gifted, created for living with greater ease and freedom . . . is fixed to perfection, to time-table, to pattern, and hides her real self in the back-ground . . . Her motto is, "I do my bit, and if you can recognize me duly I am safe and nothing can happen to me anymore." . . . so behind her good adjustment is fear and lack of courage . . . The sphere of the blood is neglected. What does she know about her likes and dislikes? The world of the instincts is far away. And also the spiritual life is excluded, because her own spirituality presupposes the acceptance of her whole personality . . . an air of dream is around her . . . This veils life to her and her to life . . . much shyness, anxiety . . . How could she, with all her gifts, come to this point? . . . the great father image guides and determines much behavior. But that does not seem enough to make this kind of living in her case. One could think that she once experienced something that disturbed the balance of her ego and almost crashed it. She may have experienced an aspect of life that was dreadful and unmerciful—a power of light or darkness which she could not bear. Maybe her ego was hurt by it so much since it was identified with the guilt for the darkness of life . . . Thus she banished darkness out of herself . . . Life and the world remained outside . . . The good thing is that the outer world will try to bring back into existence these inner forces which are almost extinguished. . . . That has hap-pened now, where she is forced into a new discussion about her inner situation.

Only much time and work made plain the meanings of this incredibly true analysis. Slowly there was revealed all the weight

I.   Max Zeller, analyst, graphologist and a founder of the C. G. Jung Institute, Los Angeles, 1957

of baggage—personal, familial, ancestral, archetypal—which was making my ship ride so low in the water. It was as if the Terrible Dream had tried to tell me how close my ship was to sinking, but I could neither see it nor face it then. Time waited until the synchronous event (described by Dr. Jung as two or more occurrences that like to happen together) of that last psychology class and its subject matter and the persons involved in it.

I have learned since then that we know much more than we know we know. It's in the depths of the unconscious first: it may be a long time before we know it consciously.

What I assumed I was, at the time of the Terrible Dream—and later on, at the time of the graphological analysis—was light years distant from what came to be revealed as the Me/I duality, i.e., my "dead and in hell and belonging to the devil" side *vs.* my patient, cautious, just, adaptable, anxious, cowardly side. These two had been arch-enemies since puberty or before. The battle had been concealed and the doors tightly closed except during the depressed time. So the poem quoted previsioned the insights that began to come with the graphological analysis and the therapeutic work that was "the new discussion about (my) inner situation."

Opening up the inner world in therapy was difficult, and the "I" resisted it strongly, as the Ego always does resist threats to its autonomy. The situation is not unlike a bitterly fought election between two strong political parties, one in power and not wanting to lose it, one not in power and wanting to win it. Thus the first year or two the I/Me struggle was mirrored in outer life responses and in dreams and fantasies. Some dream examples:

(1)
An evil male figure plotted to destroy a second male figure; an evil male figure tried to find me in a haunted house; an evil brother figure tried to shoot me.

These dreams opened the door of the negative masculine dimension in me, that power which was the devil and the bat-winged man in the Terrible Dream, that power which obviously (though not obvious to me at that time) was behind the self-denying, anxious, cautious, afraid side that had been my defense for so long. Only a month later, this dream marked a turn of the spiral:

(2)
*I could see the earth planet from outer space, and as I watched,
a part of the planet broke off from the whole and crashed down
onto the planet in order to put an end to war.*

If the first problem presented to me by the inner knower was that
of beginning to understand and ultimately to resolve the negative
masculine, this archetypal scene was reminding me that cataclys-
mic events would be necessary if my potential wholeness was to
be restored.

I am telling these events as if I understood them then! Of course
I did not. My inner vision was dim and my ways entrenched.
However, it is important to recount another dream, also about
the masculine dimension, which took much longer—several years,
in fact—to make itself clear to me:

(3)
*I am supposed to go at once to Germany for some very urgent
reason which I can't remember. I am wandering through the
halls of what seems to be a large building, searching for the
place where I am to start my trip. The unusually wide halls are
lined with small and rather trashy shops. Finally I meet an
elderly man who points out for me a sign with an arrow on it.
He tells me that it indicates the direction I should go. I turn
and go that way. Then I am walking into a large body of water,
somewhat like an indoor swimming pool. The water is clear
and clean and I begin swimming. Soon I come to a division
in the pool. On the other side, the water is foul and slimy, and
dotted with the heads of people swimming. Someone says (or I
know) that across this water is my destination. I am filled
with revulsion, yet I know I must and will go on. I take a deep
breath, dive into the dirty water, and begin swimming again.
Next I seem to be at some sort of very crowded slum area. I and
all the other inhabitants are trying to leave this place. I am
determined to go although I am afraid, because it means going
in small lifeboats through heavy bombardments. Someone con-
soles me by saying that the enemy only wastes two bombs on
each small boat, and if they miss, we are safe. I am also told*

that other parts of the city have no freedom at all, and I feel a heavy, invisible hand on my mouth. I remember small boats and an expanse of open sea in the night. Then I am swimming in dirty water and finally reach clean water. Finally, I am in a room filled with people. An experiment is being done on some machine, although the experiment involves critical social issues. I remember a tray being shoved into the machine, and on the tray are crowds of very tiny living human beings, and I know their lives are at stake. No one wants to go with the experiment but one man. He turns to me and says he is not afraid and will go on. I look at him. It is Abraham Lincoln, and his face is strong and sad.

This dream, as must be clear even to those who do not see fully the wisdom of the inner world, presented me with an outline of much of the entire Journey which lay ahead for me. Germany was the place of fascism. I had to subject the I (ego) to that inner place of imprisonment, uncleanness, bombardments, fear, and threats of death. Only so could I come to the place of possible healing of my civil war, the place where eventually I could recognize that the positive masculine dimension was ready to help all the small lives in me to survive.

As the doors began to open, the first item on the agenda was to deal with the negative masculine. We women of this century have been inheritors of our mothers' and grandmothers' sense of inferiority and thus of their attempts to compensate. This they did, far too often, by taking on the masculine dimensions modeled upon male uses of masculine dimension rather than finding their own female uses of masculine dimensions.

My relationship to my brother involved this negative masculine dimension. Dream (1) included an evil brother figure who was trying to shoot me. As I said earlier, I think I suffered withdrawal symptoms when my brother was born. I had had all the attention for three years. My brother came, and was sickly for quite a time. He had all the attention, or so it seemed. I resented him. I loved him. I looked after him, beat up bullies who picked on him. I made life difficult for him often. Temperamentally we were totally different. He loved life, seemed happy-go-lucky, refused to learn to talk until he absolutely had to, could sleep late in the mornings (which I never have been able to do), made fun of me for the "crooners" I adored in my teens, and was not drawn to bookish and musical things. I guess he threatened me socially because he seemed so at home and at peace with the usual world. I was an oddball. I felt he thought so and judged me accordingly. So in the first dream a brother was the masculine judge who did not approve of me, the female.

My mother essentially was a gypsy, dark, attractive, easy in laughter, loving, outgoing, joyful. Nonetheless a drivenness never let her be, giving her increasingly high blood pressure, giving her death from a massive cerebral hemorrhage at the age of 59. She and my father worked hard, but she was the stronger personality, and as times grew more difficult she had the office job, while he worked on street maintenance. They had the usual arguments of marriage, but their relationship was better than most, and had much love in it. Yet I remember saying to myself one day when they were struggling with the money problem and my mother was angry, that I never wanted to be like my father. My paradigm for being able to make it was my mother in her very deadly, never-say-die masculine dimensions. In me, these are pictured in the first dreams, and in the Nazi bombardment.

My disfiguring acne in my teens added to the sense of inferiority inherited from my female ancestors. This led me the next step of the way. I used my brains, scholastic achievements, and all the masculine dimensions that went with these compensations.

So how did my analyst and I work with Dream (3)? What did we do with the dirty and clean waters, the war, and the hindering and the helpful male figures? Obviously I did not want to enter into the dirty waters—into the conflicts and messinesses of moving into new dimensions of life. I had avoided the rough waters and bombardments of the inner world of the unconscious— probably because they had been so threatening to me since the Terrible Dream. So we worked to get me related somehow to the Abraham Lincoln figure—although in all truth I suppose only very recently have I come to feel in reality what it is to stay with all the little ones in the tray. It took many years for me to recognize

II.   Sheila Moon, about 1935

in myself the validity of the courageous sadness that was on Lincoln's face in that early dream. Or to accept his ugliness as my own.

I was working days and going to school nights, trying to complete a Master's program, and going on weekends with a group of friends, men and women, most of them in the same work-school pattern as I was. Yet for all of that I seemed always lonely because I felt so intensely a misfit in life. I was beset by a hauntedness, a sense of dark forces at my heels. Which indeed they were, if I reflect on the dreams of death, devil, murderers, Fascists, foul and slimy waters. I worked hard, studied hard, played hard, smoked, drank (not as much), had too little sleep. But I was increasingly concerned with the inner journey and its deeper meanings—although I walked out of analysis during the first year in a fit of classical resistance.

II

Endings and Beginnings
(1940–1944)

Between that fate-filled non-choice of my final undergraduate
class and my first trip to Europe—especially to Zurich and to the
opening of the Jung Institute—came eight turbulent years. The
spiritual search took a giant step after I attended a summer seminar called simply A Study of the Records of the Life of Jesus. All
dogma and belief were carefully and critically set aside as we
struggled to understand this incredible Jew and his teachings. It
was one of the greatest ends and beginnings in my life. This first
seminar was given in Ojai on the grounds of the Krishnamurti
center. The early dream of the planet and war (2) described not
only the world's condition then but also mine. Something of my
deepest Self would have to break from bondage and shake my
existence into peace. After my first seminar:

(4)
I am walking to the mountain place where seminars are held.
It is a long way. I am in old clothes, carrying a staff but no
baggage. My companion is an odd little dwarf woman, and we
are singing.

Feeling back into this dream, I am reminded of the scene where Ezekiel the prophet is told by God to go out with only an exile's baggage. As our individual journeys begin, we are exiles from our old countries of routine, defenses, fears. I have found no better way to discover Self-ness than this painful road of exile from the walled-in protection behind which we hide our wounds. My inner dreamer told me this:

(5)
I am walking alone in a deep forest.
A voice says, "This way is the Will of God."

This way? Darkness, lostness, aloneness? Yes. This is in fact the only route that is not preprogrammed to its end. It is the forest of Dante, Poliphilo, Goethe, as described in their visionary journeys. It is the forest of folktale and myth, where travelers are lost, where they encounter beasts, giants, sorcerers and such, and stumble by accident onto treasures undiscovered for centuries. As an example of what such treasures could be came this dream:

(6)
I am with a black woman friend, wandering through rooms filled with drawings and sketches related to books for children. One such book is dated 1861.

This is the year the Civil War started! So one meaning is clear. The date is also somewhere near my paternal grandfather's birth year. He was a very special person to me in my childhood. A retired minister, shaggy and bearded, he lived in southern California with his second wife. The year 1861 would also have been near my maternal grandmother's birth. She too was very important in my early life.

At the time of this 1861 dream (6), nothing could have been less likely to occur to me than the idea that in twenty-five years I would have published two successful children's novels. The child part of me in 1941 was almost totally covered over by the adapted, conforming, rational person. It was a long journey to find that inner child—but the inner map had the place marked.

I believe that in some queer way this first intimation of my lost inner child had to coincide with the death of my mother. Dream (6) came in July, her death in September. In another month she would have been sixty. Her style of dying was like her style of living—fast, no complaints, painted with a broad brush in bold colors.

My mother had never spoken to me (I suspect not to anyone) either of dreams or of death. A few hours before her death, we were working in her garden together. She put her trowel down and with a smile, told me she had dreamt the previous night of being pursued down an alley in darkness by dark men. We went on with the gardening. After a piece of time she laid down her tool again and asked me to stop for a bit. Very directly she said, "If I should die before your father—and I hope not, for his sake— I want . . ." and she told me what she wanted for a funeral. It was so unexpected and brief and unusual an exchange that I hardly took it in. About three hours later at my brother's home with myself, my father, my brother, my sister-in-law, my toddling nephew, all present, she died.

This shock numbed me for awhile, then split wide open the cosmic Pandora's box where all my unsolved parental problems, all my insecurities (psychological and physical), and all my harsh masculine dimension dictators had been shut away.

I had not lived in my parents' home for many years. Since I was eighteen I had shared an apartment with a friend, first in the small town where I had lived for many years with the family, had gone to high school, and had worked at an assortment of jobs. Later on when I returned to the university the friend and I moved nearer to the campus. She was sort of a child to me— attractive, youthful in manner, demanding, unpredictable, always with a new man, always distressed about something. I was always "mother"—steady, orderly, supportive, helpful, and calming. But she helped me in many ways when I went back to school and was both working and studying. Thus we were each, in different circumstances, child, mother, partner.

After my mother's death the inner turmoil of mother-daughter complex grew greater. I was unsure of my own feminine dimension and harassed by aspects of my negative masculine dimen-

III.   Sheila Moon's mother (right) and aunt, around 1895

sion. In these ways I was very like my mother. She had sacrificed her natural, joyful, free gypsy masculine dimension in order to carry the needed masculine dimension of work, work, work for the whole family. Certainly this had killed her. It was already pursuing me. I was driving myself in school, working long hours, smoking incessantly, staying up late. I was losing weight and becoming irritable and tense.

Within two months after my mother's death I dreamed:

(7)
I am in a forest, carrying a gun, trying to escape from a sinister male gunman. A drunk man is also pursuing two women. Then a vicious man attacks me in an old deserted house.

From these pieces of a dream, the danger of the negative masculine dimension is perfectly clear. The ego itself is threatened, and then arms itself with negative masculine dimension weapons. The feminine dimension is endangered also. My mother's pattern was clearly stated. Her own dream of being chased by the two dark men was echoed in my dreams.

Then, in the same period, came a dream containing clues to the eventual resolution, or beginning resolution, of the negative masculine problem, although I could only work with it much later.

(8)
I see, coming toward me from dark woods, the Spirit of Evil (as I had recently seen him portrayed in Max Reinhardt's staging of the Miracle Play). He is satyr-like, playful, and belongs to me.

The inner dreamer was trying to say then that if I could see some dark things as mine, related to my repressed instincts which wanted to be expressed playfully, this could be a miraculous redeeming of the spirit. I could not yet hear. I went on driving myself at work and at school, determined to get my Master's degree. Which I did. I was given a teaching assistantship at the University of California, Berkeley, for the following year.

This was a major shift of my life—so soon after mother's death to move away from places I had been in for twenty years, the people, the surroundings, the known world. To take up a life totally unknown in almost every dimension. In the life I left there had been several central persons apart from my family. There was the friend I had shared life with for almost twelve years. There were the few high school friends with whom I had kept in touch. There were my father, my brother and his family. There was the man to whom I had been intimately related since I was twenty. There were my good friends, Luella Sibbald and seminar leader and analyst Elizabeth Howes, introduced to me by my psychology professor. All of these people lived in one half of the state while my new job meant I would be in the other half.

My dreams kept telling me where the difficulties and dangers would be. There were scenes of wars, bombings, falling into abysses, seeing terrible disasters from machines, being lost, disorganized, ostracized. Dreams also gave me some helpers—such as frogs, seahorses, pools with purple fish and grottoes with lovely animals in them, dogs of all kinds and colors and sizes, tiny lambs, tiny wild mice in trees, and one startling dream with a black boy, a black fish, a black hummingbird, all friends. I was now aware that the inward world was somehow a corrective to the outward world, that dream and fantasy gave clues to what was needed for better balance, or to what had been destructive, or was still being destructive.

It was growing more evident to me that one of the biggest difficulties for me was my negative inner masculine which was trying to destroy me. In the few months before I left for my new job, these dream statements came:

(9)
My head was injured in a fight with a man who was beating a child; I watched a man brutally axe off the head of a young calf; a man shot, for no reason, a joyful and wild goat; a Japanese soldier abused a woman because she had tears.

On the other side of things, I kept having dreams about love and marriage and many exciting sexual dreams about men I knew (and some I did not know), so they helped me—albeit mostly unconsciously—to keep some balance.

I could not see my relationship to me clearly, and so could not act where I needed to act. Perhaps—if the man with whom I had the fullest relationship had not been considerably older, we would have married and perhaps, under the circumstances of my unconsciousness, it might have been disastrous. Who can tell? (In any event, we did come together again later, and stayed in a deep relationship until his death.)

I arrived in Berkeley filled with anxiety and dread, my insides in a chaotic state, and moved into an apartment of my own for the first time in my life. I managed to keep myself in one piece and carry out my duties as a teaching assistant adequately. Also I was preparing for the eighteen hours of comprehensive exams required of all doctoral candidates. It took time to make new friends, so the negative masculine had all the leeway in the world to disturb my dreams.

(10)
I am in a room with my mother, my former housemate, and several young men. I am beating about me with a huge club. I knock one young man to the floor. Then another youth, whom I once knew, a boy with a purple birthmark on the left side of his face, wrests the club from me. I look in a mirror, seeing that my eyes show only the whites, my face is contorted, and I know I am going crazy. A youth throws me across his shoulder like a sack. I break away, but then I go to him, wearily, like a little child, and say, "Please take me home and put me to bed." He picks me up gently in his arms and goes out the door.

(Later the same night) I walk down a street at twilight. It is a strange street, as if in a fairy tale. There is a little house like a gingerbread house. Over it is a sign saying Merry Christmas, or Greetings. Several little black bear cubs are playing by the house. From another house a small black pig comes out and bites at my heels. He frightens me. I pick up an apple, throw it into the house and, as he rushes in after it, I run and close a big metal door. Outside, in the street, suddenly a lovely male reindeer comes up to me. I climb on his back. He takes my hand

(the right one) in his mouth, biting it very gently and smiling at me. I know that if my hand isn't there we can't fly. Then we rise from the street, into the air, past windows of little houses in the narrow street, past windows with people and toys. It is terribly exciting, and I keep saying, "Oh reindeer, go higher!"

Then he suddenly begins to drop downward toward a narrow street or the opening to a dark building. He cries out, "Look out!" I look down and see ahead of us, blocking the way, a gigantic and shadowy elk, and I know he will kill the reindeer unless we do something. I begin to scream as we descend. As we swoop through the entrance or opening I see lions, tigers, bears, their heads toward us. My screams awaken me.

It is fortunate that we do not have to face such bursting messages every night! Our poor spirit and substance in their uneasy alliance could not sort them out. This time it was what I needed, when ends and beginnings seemed almost unbearable. The first dream of the night was showing me some of the ways in which I had tried to deal with my ego identity. I could bludgeon my way with my brains. I could let myself lose all control and fall apart. I could become childlike and give myself into a helper's arms as a child. The last way was right for me, because so very difficult. It led directly to the second dream—as if permitting myself to become the helpless and needy child also permitted access to the shapes and figures of the unconscious in vivid colors, shapes, lines—in the world of faerie. The little bears related to the very first story I ever read by myself, at a preschool age. The pig surely was related to repressed and cut-off lower impulses and drives, and I tried, even at this point, to get rid of it by throwing the apple (from the tree of the knowledge of good and evil) and shutting them both away.

The reindeer is a rich symbol in myth and folktale. Here it was, I feel, the animal of imaginative, creative thought, to which I had to surrender my conscious control, my right hand. As I look back, I believe that the great elk had to be faced because I tried to shut away and get rid of the pig. If we refuse the small instincts, then we are either totally cut off from all instincts or we have to encounter them in the large. Witness, lions, tigers, bears, as well as elk, all present.

The night following came a warning parental dream.

(11)
I am in an operating room, standing with others around the operating table. A woman surgeon is making a long incision in the abdomen of the patient. The patient is a strange figure, changing from mother to dad and back again. I see the figure writhing as if in pain, and the head and shoulders are my dad's. Then the surgeon is scraping intestines and blood onto the floor, and it is mother.

This was obviously a much too brutal fashion in which to try to solve the parental problems. Was the woman surgeon my own rational and cold-blooded side which wanted to cut out all life from the parents? This was partly answered by the next dream.

(12)
Something is wrong with my left foot and leg. A male doctor does something for me, then he and a woman put me on my feet and support me. I can now walk a little, but he says that I will be crippled for life. Then somewhere I get a cane belonging to Harry, a cane which I always liked, and use that to get me around.

At least there are two helpers, a man and a woman, to take care of me. Everyone is in some way crippled for life. The buried, wounded and undeveloped parts of us—together with the over-developed defenses and fortresses which guard against our feeling the wounds—cannot be there for as long as they are, for most of us, without leaving ineradicable scars. There are always places in me that are awkward places, or that produce awkward behaviors in certain situations, and it does not matter that I have journeyed for almost forty years now. They are there. They will continue to be there at times of stress, although diminished and less noticeable to anyone but me. So—in that sense some part of me is crippled for life. To accept that fact is to begin to be mature in a very real way. To realize that we cannot blame it all on our

parents is also a maturing. The sins of the fathers and mothers
are truly visited onto the children from generation to generation
—until somebody tries to make the pattern conscious and so
changes the pattern totally. If I limp a bit—so does everyone.

Dream (12) also told me that I could not fall back totally on
the way of the man who loved me (via his cane). I had to stand
on my own feet and walk on them, even though haltingly. No
man, woman, child could define my way any longer for me
except those inner men, women, and children who people my
dreams. Those I must come to know, understand, live with,
listen to, follow. For example;

(13)
*I see my little cousin Judy sliding down a steep balustrade, and
I go down a few steps and take her in my arms, cuddling her
and patting her sun-browned little bottom lovingly. Far below
us is the sea and a wide meadow. On the meadow facing the
sea is Father Hill in his vestments leading a group of people in
the Credo. I begin to say it aloud with them. In this group are
two men, a huge microcephalic and his brother, who is supporting him. Both have long hair and very hairy faces, and they
add something to the Credo about being "bound together forever by our hair."*

Certainly my little cousin Judy was a genuine feminine being,
free, naked, unashamed. As I accept her into my arms, a group
fellowship is possible, including all the aspects of the masculine
from the loving priest to the idiot brother, who is always a part
of the real Self, and is united to us eternally by his primitive and
biological realities. Only when we take him with us, slowly and
very patiently, do we really have the needed strength to proceed.
It is not come by easily, or without much suffering, many dreams,
deep struggles.

In the midst of my comprehensive exams and the necessary
sacrifice of my personal life for study and work, came another
crashing warning of how close I was getting to real collapse, both
of body and of mind.

(14)
I am in an America which is under siege by the Nazis. Bombs are being dropped around us. I look up into the sky and see that a huge net is being drawn by hundreds of dirigibles and balloons. Moving slowly and ponderously, it finally covers the whole sky. We are hemmed in by the Nazis. I realize that our army and air force are doing nothing. I go to a close friend and tell her that soon we will both probably be called before a Nazi tribunal, and that therefore we must both immediately dispose of all Russian literature which we have. I am aware of much conflict as I speak with her. First, how can America get supplies out to attack the enemy? Second, I face the terrible fact that, because I am afraid, I am going to compromise and burn my real beliefs instead of standing up for them and taking the consequences.

This dream, and another one about disastrous train wrecks, were anticipating a major crisis. The ego had balked, the intellectual values had failed, and I was being hemmed in by collective conformity and regimentation even to the point of self-betrayal. Finally came this:

(15)
I am an adopted child. My stepmother (I did not have one then) has left word that when I cannot stand things any longer I should commit suicide by drowning. I see myself entering the water and being lashed by a young man.

This sort of message resembles various folktales of the wicked stepmother whose masculine dimension is destructively directed toward the heroine of the tale, who has to go through many trials before she is rescued by some magician or prince. The story is a very real one—which is why it is found so widely distributed throughout the world.

We have inner parent figures who time and time again try to wipe us out. Sometimes our true parents did this. More often than not our inner parents are parental attitudes which we ourselves have learned to take toward our unwanted and hard-to-handle feelings, emotions, tendencies and all sort of things making us uncomfortable and anxious. As that early handwriting analysis made so clear, I had almost destroyed my creative side, my spontaneity, my willingness to risk. I had settled for a safe, secure, all-things-in-order mode of meeting life. Events had smashed through this from several directions, and I was left unprotected from the assaults of the unconscious which had for so long been imprisoned. According to dream (15) I did not know my own inner mother, but was being condemned to death by a non-parent —as if the non-parent said, "All right. If you want to mess around with the unconscious, go ahead and drown. It will be at any rate an end to suffering."

Fortunately for me, the therapist I was seeing at the time held on to me so I didn't go completely under. I had many dreams about my mother, as healthy, as ill, as demanding, as in need, and finally as dead and returning to the realm of the Mothers. Also I had a dream of my father dying in my arms. (In fact he had just remarried.) So at a very deep level matters were changing shape. I was moving away from the dependency of childhood, letting the parents go, and night after night falling in love with or being engaged to some man or being married, or having two men between whom I could not choose. This kind of inner movement is quite usual in the early phases of the Self Journey. If it weren't, few of us would make it.

One of the helpful trends had to do with the increasing number of religious dreams and the stabilizing effect they had, though I did not see much of what they meant. Let me telescope several such dreams:

(16)
A small silver cross which I hold becomes the cross of the crucifixion; a little girl comes to me and asks, "Where is God and what is He?"; I have a lovely wooden cross, jeweled, on a wooden bead chain; an old man makes and gives to me a cross, made of a branch and a cornstalk, and then I lose it; I tell a psychology professor that religion is vital, and to my surprise he agrees; I struggle all night fighting over decisions between two alternatives, and thinking about Kierkegaard and his Fear and Trembling.

At the time of these dreams, I had changed analysts due to my

IV.   Sheila Moon and her father, The Pines, 1949

change of residence from Southern to Northern California and was with one of the warmest and most human of women who probably took me through more rough water than any analyst I have been with. She saw me through stormy waters when I hardly knew how to swim, much less handle a boat. She felt that dreams such as those above were underlining for me the need to affirm the difficulties of life as part of the purpose of God, as having meaning and reason. I was beginning to feel this for myself, having experienced two summer seminars on the life of Jesus. My analyst said to me, "We have to go into the terrifying waves over and over again, and every time we do we get stronger."

In the final week of that year I had two dreams which were landmarks in the understanding of how to face and transform suffering.

(17)

I am at a performance of the opera La Forza Del Destino, *and go outdoors between acts to walk in the garden of the opera house. It is a formal garden arranged in terraces. It is a soft, dark evening. I am wandering up and down the terrace stairs. I see a man coming toward me in the night. He is in his thirties, blonde, wearing old clothes and a cap, and I see that he is a cripple, having no legs from his knees down, and no hands, only stumps. Suddenly filled with a sense of love, as we pass I reach out and lay my hand on his shoulder. I start on, but he seizes me fiercely, pulls me down, and starts beating my head against the cement stairs. I cry for help but no one is near to hear me. He is terribly powerful and I am helpless and trapped. Then I begin to pray—very quietly but audibly—"O God, please keep me from letting this experience make me bitter, or make me hate!" His arms loose me, I get to my feet, and I see him, on his knees, arms at his sides, tears streaming down his face.*

The second dream, five nights later.

(18)

San Francisco is a place of death, or pain, or suffering, and I know I must walk in it with a gnarled branch for a staff—like a branch from a great cedar tree.

The dream set in the opera garden is one of those that is as vivid today as it was then. Sometimes the inner dreamer presents us with a complete summary and possible resolution for a problem that we believe will never go away—so it was with me and this negative masculine dimension. It felt to be unconquerable, overpowering, no matter what I told myself to do and no matter what I perceived to be the falsity of it. It tyrannized me in situation after situation, reducing me to an angry, inarticulate, frustrated nothing.

From this dream forward I had a different attitude toward the problem of my fate. The *forces of destiny*—this was the opera, the opus, the work within which this turnabout occurred. Never was the wounded nature of this poor masculine creature more clear. No feet, no hands, nothing with which it could move forward easily or handle its environment. Poor wretch. For so long he had suffered so, been humiliated, scorned, by my arrogant ego. No wonder he wanted to tear that ego to pieces. It was only I (ego) who could alter the situation—by unbidden love, by not wanting to be embittered or hateful regardless of the hurting. This prayer went with me for months. I remembered it so vividly that in many situations where I felt the self-denying, cruel, suicidal masculine dimension begin to take over, I could—and did—repeat the prayer of the dream. It frequently helped me lessen the inner rage and self-flagellation. Sometimes I could even begin to stop it almost before it began. Sometimes I couldn't, of course. Growth and change lie along bumpy roads.

Unquestionably the "destiny" dream (17) helped me to work with the truth of the second one (18). San Francisco was the place where the tidy routine life of the past had died, and where the pain and the suffering of reality—rather than of egocentricity—had to be both learned and then endured as necessary. I had to walk with my own staff. The "mother" had died literally.

The negative masculine figures kept coming to confront me and to remind me that I was far from free.

(19)
A small green robot came dancing into a room, danced out and

returned full-sized, fantastic and threatening. I said to someone
"His name is Terror!"
Then I am with a small urchin boy, and a grotesque dwarfish
man comes in. He is ugly, with a large head and jagged teeth,
and he wraps his arms around the child and is trying to destroy
him. I point my arm toward him and say, "I am the moon
goddess." The two figures change slowly, the grotesque one
becoming a flaming sun head with rays and with arms gently
around a beautiful blonde boy with closed eyes.

Despite the presence of Terror as a huge mechanical Thing, and
the ugly dwarf (who seems to carry over from the Destiny dream
(17)), I had at last come to a place where I could begin to get in
touch with the deep feminine moon aspects of myself. Certainly
the transition from Terror to Moon and Sun archetypes jumped
far beyond where I was, and yet the possibility of changes from
negative to positive was present.

My inner dreamer decided then to present me with a classic
Jekyll-Hyde dream:

(20)
There are two of me—an A personality in a wine-red housecoat,
long hair falling over my face, down on its knees in front of a
B personality in a dark robe, very wild hair, eyes violent and
psychotic. I, as A personality, seem to be seeing the scene in a
mirror. B personality has A personality in a violent grip with
intent to kill. I, as A personality, feel I must fight back but seem
utterly unable to move. Then, as A personality, at last I seem
to be struggling with B personality, who has a gun pointed at
me (A personality). Finally I succeed in turning the gun in B
personality's hands toward B personality. I feel it goes off and
shoots B personality.

So the battle between myself and my negative inner other was
beginning to surface. My analysis helped me see it more clearly,
stating where the B personality operated, and be more ready
to tackle it. I could see, to my great consternation, how near to a
schizoid split I had let myself come. Or the gods had pushed me.
Or my chosen journey had taken me. The main fact was that here
I was, and I hadn't gone off the deep end yet. I knew without

doubt that there was a way to go to my true self. That summer
I went again to a seminar on the life and teachings of Jesus; Kunkel and Howes now had their own grounds in the San Bernardino
mountains. I also attended seminars by Dr. Fritz Kunkel at the
same place—thus exposing myself more and more to the psychological-religious way—not at all that of organized religion but of
Kunkel, Jung and the basic teaching of Jesus, relatively unknown
to Christianity. Fritz Kunkel was from Berlin. A German professor
and psychologist, he had recently been spirited out of Germany
by receiving an appointment to teach a year at the Pacific School
of Religion. Soon the rest of his family followed, first his wife
and later their children.

Kunkel was a delight. He was short and impish and twinkled
whenever he told stories. One such time was when he told us
of his twin brother who had lost an arm in the war, and as Kunkel
had lost the other arm, he would say, ". . . and do you know it
is very economical, we only had to buy one pair of gloves."

During the following few months the dreams presented me
with some very helpful themes and variations on themes having
to do with the journey and ways it could be deepened. Among
them was one of the most awesome and mysterious dreams I've
ever been invaded by:

> (21)
> *I am in or around an old mysterious house. A voice tells me to
> do as the Chinese or the Indians do—something about placating
> the ancestors, disposing of all their possessions, and other rites.
> I open a door in the earth, at the base of the house outside.
> Down in a deep hole are dome-like containers for ashes of dead
> ancestors. As I peer down, a wind rushes up and a fearful
> unseen presence clutches me by the throat and says "Murder!
> Murder!" I reach for my cross—I can't find it, but I make a ges-
> ture of throwing it down the hole, close it over, and flee.*

The terror of this dream lasted for many months. Even now,
in remembering what I felt when I awakened with it, I am filled
with dread and the desire to run from it. When I told it, the
analyst said firmly, "We will not deal with this now. You are not
ready for these ancestral evils yet." Then he added, "You made

V. Fritz Kunkel, 1948

VI. The Pines, Southern California, early 1950s

VII.   Maternal grandmother, mid-1890s

VIII.   Paternal grandmother, mid-1890s

the ancient religious gesture, which is enough.''

He meant it, and even though I was startled, I sensed then (and feel today) that he was right. I'm not sure even today that I know what the dream meant. It was impossible not to connect it with what the graphologist said a few years before: "She may have experienced an aspect of life that was dreadful and unmerciful—a power of light or darkness which she could not bear. Maybe her ego was hurt by it so much since it was identified with the guilt for the darkness of life . . .''

What this something was I have never learned and probably will never learn. I know only that there have been at least three suicides in my ancestral past. What *does* one experience in childhood? Even in infancy? I know only that I was born on Christmas Day in a Catholic hospital during such a fierce blizzard that the heating system broke down, and my father could not reach the hospital, and I was carried around during the first hours of my life by nuns holding me to keep me warm. These events in themselves hold incredible opposites of life and death, of darkness and birth and rebirth. My mother could not nurse me because of a breast infection, and I was allergic to cow's milk. More opposites. So who is to say that somewhere in my ancestral past there are not mysterious events. Even to the cry of Murder. No one of us anywhere in the world can be sure there is not murder somewhere in our past—not when we are the inheritors of the terrible history of our destruction of one another for land, for goods, for anger and for God.

III

Breaking Apart (1945–1947)

At the end of my second year in Berkeley, working as a teaching assistant and trying to complete my Ph.D., I was hospitalized for what was diagnosed as recurrent rheumatic fever, which ended for the time being my sporadic university career. After I left the hospital I returned for a time to Los Angeles where I began work as a psychotherapist.

I see the time between my return to San Francisco a year later and my first trip to Zurich in 1948 as a time of breaking apart. It felt as if all of the values of my life were turned upside down, cracked open like eggs, and as if I were continually trying to hold these open raw eggs in my hands. There's nothing essentially wrong with eggs in this condition, except that they are messy unless you have a dish handy. As yet I hadn't. It took me quite a time to get one. This dream pushed me hard.

(22)
Some man is trying to show me how to use a queer measuring gadget—something you sight through and tell distances and directions. I tell him I know about this, and he seems impressed.

*I begin to look at different things through it. I am sitting on a
sort of porch on a narrow street. Across from me are buildings
with balconies up two or three stories. Was it called the Street
of Harlots? I look through this gadget to a balcony above. There
is a large, black and orange, Gay Nineties lamp there, and a
woman beside it. As I look, it is as if my looking causes the
lamp to fall to the street and smash. A woman comes down and
says to me, "Tomorrow Athens, and you will have to meet this
then." I am in anguish over what I have done. I am holding
a cedar branch.*

I associated the color black and orange with my parents (especially with my mother) because Hallowe'en was their wedding
anniversary, and always on that day they had a big party. Mother
loved decorating the house with bats and cats and witches and
colorful festoons of these colors. By looking through this instrument, whatever it was, I had "killed" something related to her
and these memories. The woman who spoke to me was like a high
priestess from Greece, and the cedar branch was the same mystical staff for journeys I had dreamed of before. Another facet of
this dream was that for once I did not run away from the consequences of my action. I was deeply distressed but used none of
the ways out that I had used in the past. I had tried so hard for
so long to be a "good daughter," putting down my angers and
frustrations, indulging my addictions as escapes from such reality
as this dream portrayed. Here I accepted my deed.

Another dream showed a growing acceptance of myself as
I was:

(23)
*There are people standing near me and laughing at my face
because it is so ugly. I am very sad, but try to explain to them
that I cannot help it.*

Contained in this dream was also the reason why I could now
begin to feel love for the ugly Abraham Lincoln.

Then came another one of the experiences such as the graphological analysis I discussed earlier in which I was again described
vividly by a person who did not then know me. We met briefly
at a professional gathering. Like the graphologist, she too was

a refugee from Nazi Germany. After this first meeting I dreamed
that she said a basic problem for me was "feeling and the family."
Then I asked her, with some misgivings, if she would do a hand
analysis for me. After a careful study of handprints and of hand
postures these were the comments she made, as nearly as I could
get them down.

A striking childhood separation from reality. Seems to have
been a trauma at about 2 years. Childhood situation—of being
walled off from life—seems to have persisted until at least 12
years. She was almost lost from the real world. The "I" was relatively nonexistent. Father or mother, or both, were completely
split between conscious and unconscious. The unconscious was
left empty, cut off. One, or both, were tied to tradition and
convention, were rigid and rational. Also were indecisive and
vacillating. One had a real sexual problem. As a very young child
she was completely at the mercy of the environment, and developed a very strong moral responsibility, giving in and giving up
on everything. This persisted up to about thirty years. [I was then
thirty-five.] Beginning in her twenties there was some break-
through of individuality. And a human relationship developed
which acted as a catalyst, bringing alive her feeling and her
intuition.

[As to Jungian type, she put me, quite accurately, as sensation
and thinking dominant.] But the intellect is not a hindrance.
Intuition is weak, limp, uncertain, but does cooperate well with
thinking. It is coming more alive now. Feeling is alive and
present, not blocked, but the problem is to experience life and
people by both thinking and feeling. There is much feeling power
and energy—but the split has sometimes been almost schizoid.

The deep childhood trauma caused emotional infantilism and
much unreality. Sex has been extremely repressed, although her
sexual reactions are alive and received but cut off. Because of
this, there has been much lack of courage for human relationships, and many opportunities have been lost. The shadow problem has been great, and feared, and because of this there has
been repression, perfectionism, and romanticism. Her personal
way has not been established. She has been too adjustable and
indecisive. ("You are one of the few who can really assimilate
your shadow," she said to me emphatically, "but it takes faith

and courage.'') The animus is deeply buried. ''Have you ever really talked with him?'' There has always been a depressive trend, a self-destructive tendency, which could be partly masochistic but also truly suicidal. The imagination has not been well-developed. Much tension and lack of energy.

Very positive hand as to gifts. A good balance between introversion and extraversion. Very psychic—almost clairvoyant. Receptive, sensitive hand, impressionable, a moulder's hand. Good instincts and sensual eros, but blocked. Active and dynamic drive is natural and potential but not realized yet. An educator's talent, maternally expressed. Sense of the dramatic in life and art. Highly developed unconscious, which is at a high level of growth. Very far ahead of the persona, which is too rational and slow. Follow the unconscious. It is creative, connected, wise. A good analyst. Unconscious well related to reality.

This study helped me a great deal in this period of breaking apart. It showed me that all of my weaknesses were not of my own invention, but part of the package. It aided my self-acceptance. It laid open the parental problem. It helped me to see why relationships had been so difficult, on the whole. It gave me hope for the future, at a time when hope was definitely not ''a thing of feathers'' perched in my soul but something which I felt alienated from. It helped me to be ready for a dream that came a few months later:

(24)
I am with some relatives and some friends in a room. Pushing up through the floor comes a stalk of a large plant. It grows very rapidly. Its tip is a blossom which becomes a red-haired little boy. As it grows it withers and shrivels as if from heat, and the child's hair flames, crackles, and wilts. I say, ''Here is what I don't like about certain aspects of religion.'' (I am thinking of the parables of Jesus about seeds and poor soil.) Slowly up pushes a large dark-red-brown mast. It grows and grows, reaching the ceiling. On its tapered end is a gold cross. I take it up. It is large and heavy, and so tall that I have to carry it slanted to get it into the next room. There I show it to people. I say, ''I can't explain this, how it came to be or why, I only know it is right and sound.'' They seem filled with wonder.

The first growth was a poor weed one, related somehow, I believe, to that misdirected intensity of my mother which drove her—and was near to driving me (or in fact had, as my illness indicated)—to collapse, being consumed by fire. The second growth was entirely different. As a ship's mast it was related to the unconscious water world. Surely, it was for me to carry, and also for me to accept without rational explanations. It was also a rich comment on my changing religious attitudes. Not until I was introduced to the synoptic teachings of Jesus—and also to the richness of the depth psychologies of Kunkel and then of Jung— did I find religious meanings in events of my life. Only thus could I come to the place where I could carry the mast with the cross and feel sure that it was right and sound, although I didn't know why.

Three days later came another crucial dream of a very different sort. I had met an older man in one of Kunkel's seminars and had come to know him as a person. Not intimately, but I felt strongly drawn to him. He was gifted and immersed in the occult world of psychic phenomena. Thus he touched me at the place where, according to the hand analysis, I too was gifted but had never honored that gift. The dream:

(25)
A man is coming to see me. It is _____. I know I love him and he loves me and we are to be together. He arrives. I point him out to a friend, and say how fine he is. He doesn't look like _____, being stronger in build, and somewhat younger. Then his wife is there. She is sorrowing because she is to lose him. I console her, my arm about her. Yet it seems destined to be so. (The whole feeling of the dream was heavy, fateful, sad.)

The inner dreamer seemed to be telling me I was destined to be related to this highly intuitive and psychic animus. This destiny involved a letting go of the overcautious maternal bonds with which I had kept intuitiveness tied down. It must grow up and be really a partner in love. My too-present "earth wife" had to be replaced by the right relationship to the spiritual masculine who was to come.

For the rest of this year I was bombarded with devastating dreams. I fought to keep my balance both for my own sake and for my professional work as therapist. My only help was by way of visits to and telephone conversations with my Berkeley analyst, bless her infinite patience! The most important dream of this period was this:

(26)
I am at the bedside of an old lady who is dying. A few death throes and she is dead. Then I have her in my arms, very aware of her head against my shoulder and her legs over my arm. I seem to be trying to find a place for her body. I wander into a high society wedding, where someone is playing a ukelele. But I go on, carrying her and weeping and weeping, feeling that my tears are the redemption for the old woman.

I had never quite fully accepted and let go of the death of my mother. I had been too pressed unconsciously by the sense of having to live her unlived life. Perhaps also she represented all of my past, its sadness, its deprivation, its limited quality. Again my analyst's wisdom helped me embrace my pain: "You have literally to sweat it out, to stay with it, to carry the old one and weep for her. Stop trying to extravert away from it in any way. There is only one possible method for meeting these awful moments and that is to sit down with them and take them in your arms until they are redeemed."

In these years of the breaking apart, I began to learn that the unconscious carefully presents us with certain recurring symbols, as if they were talismen for the learning of our own inner secrets. No two people, I have found, have the same cluster of symbols, and yet each unique cluster is made up of ancient symbols used by inner dreamers down through the centuries of human history. For example, already I have mentioned dreams with the cedar staff in them. There are subsequent ones. I have also described several dreams of deep and very troubled waters, sometimes sea, sometimes not. This symbol has always been one of the most frequent and most important, as will be seen later. Another is that of the Fool—and in the beginning I would never have believed this would prove to be such a vital part of my Self. But it is. It stood, at first, as the counterpoise to my depressed and solemn being, only showing itself quickly and disappearing as quickly again. It came clearly, in its first real appearance, as follows:

(27)
I become angry at two policemen who accuse me of something I did not do, saying that was why people hated cops. Then I am alone in a strange dim place of water, rocks, lily pads. I have to move furniture and other things across a lake or river. I find a two-wheeled cart and take it along. I also meet a little man in a strange white mask, and he is the King of the Faeries. He helps me to load the cart and get it across. We also pull a boat with us. I tell people about him. I am also carrying his jester's sticks, charms, a carved wooden man and woman like puppets.

The same night:

(28)
My brother told me that, the night before, he and my father had found me leading two horses into my cabin. They had followed me in, knowing I was walking in my sleep. There I talked and acted toward the horses in a strange and alarming way. I felt he meant in a sexual way, although he did not say so.

In some strange fashion these two dreams seemed to mark the turning point in my inner work although I cannot say why. Surely the coming of the Fool must have, inwardly at least, lightened the burdens somewhat, and made the carrying (and dropping) of eggs easier. My inner "parental" judge immediately moved in and tried to eliminate the Fool. In part the judge was successful but, thank God, in another part he was not. My Fool would not go entirely away. The mere fact that he was there, as I see it now, probably helped the breaking apart not to be so catastrophic as to wipe me out.

The years 1946 and 1947 were fraught with demands from life for changes so shattering that there were times I wondered if it was possible to meet them. Dreams of earthquakes, of long and difficult journeys across deserts, and of criminal characters trying to break into my home, and of deciding to commit suicide were countered by dreams of meeting a strange but wonderful man and being sought by him, and of living in new and strange worlds. One dream seems to combine both the minus and the plus of things.

(29)
I am suddenly in a play. I haven't rehearsed for it, but it seems as if I knew the lines because I had seen the play before. I have no costume and have to wear my own clothes. I get through the first act all right, although feeling uncertain and making up lines sometimes. Then, while scenes are being changed, I realize I don't know what comes next at all. A woman director, rather stern, says I'm doing fairly well but should do better. Then I try to find a copy of my part, but cannot. I know my next entrance is up a spiral ladder, to follow a criminal. A young man shows me how to go—through basements and corridors to the staircase. Then I have to climb up a very narrow spiral ladder. Someone says to me, "That's a very rugged climb!" The young man says, "Yes, it takes rugged people in this business." Then I have climbed up, waiting my entrance. I know I don't know my lines, that I may blow it, but that I'll just have to respond spontaneously if I can, and pick up cues as I go. I realize that my best friends are in the audience and think it is too bad they should have to see this.

It was a rugged way—and visible to others! Like juggling eggs. There was so much to be encompassed. One of my friends was plunged into a psychic crisis which required much steady support from me for a long time. I was carrying on a fairly good-sized practice as a psychotherapist. I was working with seminars. I was in intensive analysis myself. I had meetings to attend.

The outer changes were great, but the inner ones were where the stress was. Two dreams, far apart in meaning but close in time, show how polar some of the opposites were.

(30)
I cross a wide expanse of landscape, and see a huge barn with a great open hayloft. One of the people I am with needs help of some sort. A figure in light robes comes from the barn loft to the path beside us as a guide. It is Jesus.

(31)
A group of us are settling in a great valley. One kind of creature living there is called a "limpset" or a "palimpset." They were helpful creatures. (At that time I did not know the word "palimpsest," and had to be told there was such a word and what it meant.) But there was also a malicious, dangerous, tiny creature, like a tiny man, on the loose. He had to be caught and imprisoned. We did this, putting him in a box of mud with only his head out. He tried to get free but could not. Two different father figures gave poor excuses as to why they could not go for the police, so I decided to go, although the little man kept trying to persuade me to set him free.

The first dream said that deep spiritual help comes from the least expected place—the old hayloft. It represented the upset of all my thirty-six years of false adaptation. A barn is strong, old, weathered, rooted deep in the past, warm, a place where births happen. In imagining what else was there, I saw a warm, old, golden corduroy coat, sweet stacked hay, a mother cat with kittens, and when I imagined going inside, the half-light danced with golden motes. It was safe there, lonely but friendly. Pieces of harness were there, too, smelling of old leather and animals. The "palimpset" creatures were, of course, the "palimpsest" creatures— a palimpsest is something that has been written on twice, the earlier writing having been erased, in part or totally, to make room for the second writing.

How enormously exciting the inner dreamer is. It knows so much more than "I," using its knowledge in the right places. I needed creatures erasing the past, making space for new writings. The dangerous, tiny, malicious little man was the sneaky little animus bent upon plotting against my domain. Only I myself could get him to a place of confinement. No outer father figures would do.

The next year was incredibly filled with ups and downs. Outer ones—particularly in relationships—and inner ones that were vast and challenging in scope. Friends needed everything I could give of loving help. My living arrangements were dissatisfying. On the positive side, I made my first trip to the east coast and

gave a successful seminar on myths. This was a great adventure
for someone who had traveled little.

I will telescope a series of dreams to give some sense of what
was happening:

(32)
*I am to be initiated into an Indian tribe. I walk up a line of
Indians in some sort of bizarre dress. The white man who has
been instrumental in getting me initiated, asks if I really want
to go through it. I say I do. I bow and touch the fingertips of
the chieftain, and then of an Indian woman. I change clothes
with her. She is my initiator then, and we go together to room
after room, each time lying down, face down, heads together,
while she chants in a strange tongue. The end of the ceremony
is when I don a sort of crude stole, my hair becoming like
branches of a tree, and enter blindfolded before many people
while more rites take place, regarding certain objects which
are now mine—a ball which opens again and again each time
to reveal a smaller ball, a lovely silver frame for one of my
paintings. Then I see the Indians, looking like a band of gypsies, leaving down a narrow cobbled street in two wooden
carts, each pushed by an animal. The Indians are lurching
along joyously and carefree. Everyone seems happy. At the end
everything falls apart after the Indians leave—with my friends
accusing me of not being sensitive to their relatives, and others
accusing me of trying to cash a bad check, etc.*

I came face to face with a deep archetypal symbol that had
been with me from childhood, one that became a central theme
in my seminars and in two books I wrote later on.* I gave a seminar on Navajo myths for the first time in 1945. Native American
myths and the rich religious and artistic heritage we have from
the American Indians, North and South, are centrally meaningful
to me. So this dream initiation was unforgettable. Woman for

---

*Editor's Note: *A Magic Dwells, A Poetic and Psychological Study of
the Navaho Emergence Myth.* Middleton, Wesleyan
University Press, 1970. *Changing Woman and Her
Sisters* soon to be published by The Guild for Psychological Studies Publishing House, San Francisco.

the first time on my native soil—Woman and Earth—I was given wholeness within wholeness, and my own creativity was honored. This "native" part of me was joyous and relaxed and carefree! My whole negative accusing side moved in and tried to ruin it all. However, I have never been able to lose this dream.

(33)
I see a man in dark robes. He throws a knife which pierces deep into my back. I fall. He leaves me, and I feel I will die. I realize this is a holy war. After a long time he returns and draws out the knife, which is agonizing pain. I see him, then, as in a vision, in flowing robes like some great saint or mystic. He is kneeling in prayer. I don't know if I will live.

(34)
I was with many women, all needing help because of weakness and dissociation. I seem to be helping them from one place to another. Then I see a big, old solitary, black dog lying near the curb on the street. I go to him, sort of lying beside him and putting my arm over him gently. He lets me. Finally he gets up and we go on together, my hand buried in his fur. As we go, I pray for those who need help, and it seems as if the dog's presence was healing.

The man robed like a monk in dream (33) stated, I am sure, the pain of the "holy war" of real sacrifice—without falling into the negative repression of the deep hurts of the journey. Dream (34) was a most comforting description of the wise, quiet, old, latent, instinctual intuition of the animal, the "we shall see" attitude, without hurry and without guilt for not hurrying.

(35)
I step out of a cottage in the woods, seeking for something which was some part of me. It feels like moonlight. The ground of the meadow around the cottage is wet with dew, except for a dry and perfect circle of meadow just in front of the door. I know I must step into this, as if it were magical. I do.

This dream was a wonderful help to me. As the analyst said, "This is the magic circle of expanding consciousness, rich and fertile and not only in the unconscious." This sort of dream, when it comes, helps in the darker times when everything seems to be wrong, and all the eggs are slipping from your hands. This dream was so individual, so *mine—my* cottage, *my* meadow, *my* moonlight, *my* circle—yet none of it mine at all, but belonging to the One Who rules over magic.

(36)
I had to return alone to a high place by climbing a difficult and precarious ladder. I could see the tower-like structure, and knew I must make it, but alone. I was walking in snow, and people were laughing at me because I was so tired and weak. I had on heavy gloves to protect my hands while climbing, but I kept losing them. I approached the rope ladder, wondering if my strength would let me make the climb, and let me squeeze through the narrow opening at the top. (When I awoke my first association was of the ladder leading upward to the Father in the Navajo myth.)

(37)
I saw on a shelf a second set of me—my skin, complete from head to foot. It was lying with its back toward me. I touched it, very hesitantly and rather repelled. My finger sunk into it. It felt dead, and yet not quite. I thought, "Well, I guess you could get into it, although it would be hard, but there might be times you'd want to wear it."

Reflecting what is required of us, these dreams are definitely related to the ultimate journey of the Self. We never know if we can make it until we get there. Taken seriously these dreams show there is always that pull to one's past skins, that fatal desire to wear once again what one had worn before. A very subtle invitation to let go of the ladder.

IV

Wanderjahr
(1948–1949)

Europeans once had a custom of seeing that a young person (more often male than female) could have a *wanderjahr,* a period of months of traveling through various countries, learning about the cultures, relating to the people of the countries—in short, becoming "educated." Many members of today's younger generation have found ways of doing this as exchange students, as members of the Peace Corps, or just as wanderers with packs on their backs and general good will in their hearts.

Having been born a bit too early for the Peace Corps or wandering ways, and having not been born with a silver spoon in my mouth, I had not been to Europe until 1948 which was the first Great Year for me. There were so many firsts: planning the trip with my two close friends; traveling across the continent by train, loaded with luggage; our crossing on the *Queen Elizabeth:* crossing Europe by train so soon after World War II, England and the continent still with the terrible scars of war; Zurich which I will elaborate on shortly; Italy, especially Milan, Florence, and Sienna; recrossing the Atlantic, this time on the *Queen Mary;* recrossing the United States and arriving back in San Francisco on a balmy June night and feeling it was good to be home.

Zurich was particularly special. It was my primary destination and turned out to be so timely. Through a friend in California we learned that the Jungian Institute was just being formed in Zurich and that our trip would be coincidental with its opening.

We participated in classes with Toni Wolff, Emma Jung, Barbara Hannah, Marie-Louise von Franz, C. A. Meier and Linda Fierz. Jung was not teaching at that time but did give a few lectures. When the Institute had its formal opening with a banquet, we were there along with others who were taking and giving courses at the Institute. There were only a few Americans there. The three of us and John Perry and his wife. We had comradeship with them and also with some of the English people. One of the old-timers came to us as Americans and asked that one of us sit at Dr. Jung's table. Suddenly, I found myself at his table and it was both a delight and hysterically funny as Dr. Jung entertained us all with ribald stories the entire evening.

I was placed next to Dr. Jung and we were all asked around the table what we would like to drink and when it came my turn, I asked for some Kümmel (a German aperitif flavored with caraway seed and anise). He turned to me and said, "Mein Gott, I never knew an American who knew what it was." So he called the waitress over and I had my Kümmel.

He told us stories, one of how he guaranteed himself privacy in his home which was typical of the kind of dinner conversation that ensued. It seems that he has a special recipe for Limburger cheese dressing—very strong, and he made lots of it and ate it all and then he said he had his 48 hours of peace and quiet.

The first dream I had when I came to Zurich, before I had seen anyone analytically was the following:

(38)
I was going to see Dr. Jung and dropped my horoscope at his feet.

I worked first with Toni Wolff and found her fascinating, maddeningly perceptive and both gifted and difficult.

My initial dreams in the Old World—in London and in Zurich —were fundamental to my needs.

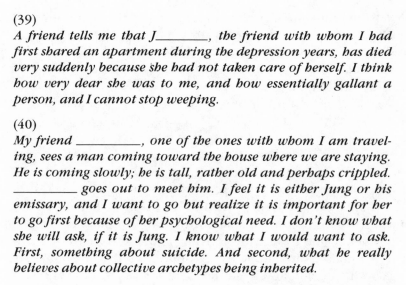

(39)
*A friend tells me that J_____, the friend with whom I had
first shared an apartment during the depression years, has died
very suddenly because she had not taken care of herself. I think
how very dear she was to me, and how essentially gallant a
person, and I cannot stop weeping.*

(40)
*My friend _____, one of the ones with whom I am travel-
ing, sees a man coming toward the house where we are staying.
He is coming slowly; he is tall, rather old and perhaps crippled.
_____ goes out to meet him. I feel it is either Jung or his
emissary, and I want to go but realize it is important for her
to go first because of her psychological need. I don't know what
she will ask, if it is Jung. I know what I would want to ask.
First, something about suicide. And second, what he really
believes about collective archetypes being inherited.*

Dream (39) presented me with the ultimate religious statement
of *let go!* To mourn, *to honor a passing by tears* is a religious act.
I think this is what Jesus meant when he said "Blessed are they
that mourn." Only in this way, perhaps, can we pay tribute to
something that has gone, whether the something is a relationship
or an attitude or a whole way of life. We cannot just cast it aside
as if it had not been. The dream (40) about Dr. Jung (or his emissary) also put into perspective what could have gotten out of
focus. The dream statement was somewhat ridiculous: Both of
my questions are answered in one or another of Jung's writings
so why did I want to ask them? My friend is one of the most
deeply religious people I have ever known, and she should have
gone first because she would ask the religious questions—which,
as we soon learned, were the questions Jung most wanted to
discuss. Perhaps I needed to honor my questions.

As I review my dreams from those six months they seem mun-
dane, although Miss Wolff and I worked hard in my analysis.
During that first stay in Zurich, I experienced the European
continent deeply and spiritually. Always gripped by the religious
aspects of life, and having found what I was seeking in my studies,
I arrived in Europe as a child open to see the fabled churches in

all their beauty and anonymity, to see the paintings of the late Byzantine and early Renaissance, to be completely swept away by the works of Michelangelo and Fra Angelico and the unknown artisans who had erected the cathedrals for the love of God. I also established an abiding relationship to the Virgin as an ultimate expression of the feminine archetypal dimension—first through a visit to Einsiedeln, a village not far from Zurich, where one of the loveliest of Europe's "black virgin" statues lives in a fabulous baroque monastery church. Since then I have visited Her countless times, as well as other "black virgins" of Europe. All of them hold the same mysterious power of the earth spirit.

I owe my sanity to my studies and to Jung's psychological approach, the most religious of all psychologies of depth. Jung himself was immersed in the spiritual nature of the human struggle. Always in our personal conferences with him, my friends and I would arrive at the point of God.

This is not to say that all Jungians share the same feelings as Jung, although religion means much in the work of Linda Fierz, Wickes, Whitmont, Edinger, Neumann, Adler, Meier—to name only a few of the better known Jungians.

To return for awhile to my Zurich *inner* journey: After dream (40) about Jung came this one:

(41)
A young woman college friend of mine and I are in a strange house as captives of a blonde feminine-looking Nazi woman jailer. A terrible and bloody battle is taking place between her and us. She violently and with amusement hits one of us. I strike her in the face with all my strength. She hits my young friend. I beat her over the head with a sheer and savage will to live surging through me. She seems to go on untiringly. I wish for a gun, realizing that tyrants have to be killed and feeling a deep empathy for those who assassinate tyrants. It is all very terrible, and she goes on taunting us, between blows, with our future fate, as if we were to be handed over to the SS men or to Hitler himself. Finally the battle lets up for a few moments and I get my young friend out into the night for a few moments' respite. I give her water from a sponge. I urge her to try to escape

up the mountain to her family's house to wait for her husband.
She is hesitant and fearful and I too am afraid—but I say, "We
must think of your husband and he is going to need you."
Finally she sneaks off into the darkness. I return to the woman
jailer who sits leering at me like a cat with a trapped mouse.
I fear she will know the girl has gone, and wonder if I should
try bribery, or confess something so the girl's escape is more
sure. But I don't trust her.

This dream was an excellent and dreadful one with which to
begin a new stage of the inner journey. As Miss Wolff and I
worked on it in analysis we saw that it described the struggle to
free the young introverted artistic feeling side of me from the
tyranny of repression and negative masculine dominance. The
conditioning of the past difficult months had to be broken so that
I could be myself. The dream told me that the ego was strong
enough. My real feelings should prepare for this change. It was a
religious one. Toni Wolff had said, "Christianity is a high moral
achievement, but religious individuation stands above it."

(42)
I'm in a large hall at night. I am with a group, sitting in a circle
around a small raised platform, also circular, in the middle of
which is a small Christmas tree with tiny candles on it. Someone
sets fire to it ritually because this is a ceremonial burning to
mark the end of some season. During the burning I am sitting
on some man's lap, feeling warm and contented there as we
watch the fire. Then a procession of singers come to herald some
new thing. Someone plays a hand organ.

This is so clearly a celebration both of my actual birth and childhood and of a second birth—that brings new fire, transformation
and initiation—as happens in European festivals when winter is
burned and the fiery sun of spring is rekindled.

A few nights later I dreamed:

(43)
I am struggling deeply through the problem of transformation.
I had an image of literally shedding or pulling off an old skin.
As a snake does. And I thought, in the dream, both of the Navajo

IX.   Linda Fierz in her yard, Kusnacht, late 1940s

hoop ceremony of rebirth, and of Jesus's statement about selling
all for the pearl of great price.

This emphasized the "rebirth" motif of dream (42) and the symbolism of my own skin being shed, as in dream (37) where I was
still toying with the idea of putting on the old one sometimes.

Linda Fierz and I became quite close and it was with her that
I had my first inclinations to work on my book about myths, *A*
Magic Dwells. The two of us became very much en rapport; we
shared interest and ideas and also she had always wanted a
daughter. She had had four sons and she sort of took me on as
a daughter.

The last dream I had before leaving Zurich was filled with a
meaning that, at the time, I could not fully comprehend.

(44)
I am carrying in my hands a very tiny baby elephant, trying
to keep it warm while I find its mother. Evidently I do find her
because later on I see the baby with its mother, both of them in
a pool of warm water, just their heads out. The baby is white,
the mother grey. Both accept me because I helped the baby
earlier. The baby is now about my size and comes and puts its
forefeet on my shoulders as an embrace. Then I tell it to return
to the water where it will be warm. Something at the end of the
dream—like a thought or an interior voice—about the size of
archetypes not being important. One must deal with them in a
real way.

I love elephants, love to watch them, feel them to be highly
intelligent and wise. In Zurich, the positive psychological and
religious meaning of elephants had been discussed in seminars
with Mrs. Fierz and with Dr. Meier. In the main lecture room
at the Institute hung a painting of one of the chakras of Kundalini yoga, a marvelous archetypal elephant with, as I recall, two
trunks. Also I had spent many hours at the Zurich Zoo watching
a baby elephant with reddish fuzz on its head go into and out of
its pool. Clearly, elephant is a positive and rich symbol for me—
of a wonderful "other," wise, patient, loving, playful, and
ancient (as Ganesa, carrier of the Buddha). Dream (44) was an

auspicious one with which to leave Zurich.

The outer sights of Europe enriched my life in many ways, giving me a sense of the architecture and art that are part of my background somewhere, grounding me in the folk customs from deep mythic lore. All the concerts and operas in Zurich were feasts to me: *Parsifal,* the Zurich festival of the burning of Winter (*Boog*) and the Basel festival of the *Morgenstreich,* a mysterious and awesome spectacle that eclipsed all others. The museums of Zurich, London, and Florence, with their treasures of the centuries, overpowered me with richness.

During all this travel and sightseeing my unconscious was responding deeply. I had dream after dream of ancient cities, great cathedrals, statues of the Virgin, Stonehenge, children like Angelico angels, beautiful statues.

Going home to San Francisco jolted me back to reality, to the push of things to be done, the work waiting, the needs to be met, and above all the realization that all wounds were not healed.

During 1949 I worked hard at seminars and at my own practice as psychotherapist. I was president of the Analytical Psychology Club of San Francisco, and I was again working to satisfy requirements for my doctoral degree.

Because the recorded dreams unearthed from that period are so few, I put some together here to give a general picture of what was going on inside:

(45)
I am with Miss Wolff and friends. We seem to have much in common. Then the Queen arrives, a strong figure who climbs to a high peak to look out over her kingdom.

(46)
I am on board a ship, with friends. But I am lost from them. And I have lost my luggage, lost my bird, and all the lights go out. Lostness and loneliness pervade everything.

(47)
An acquaintance of mine, interested in occultism, is insane.

(48)
My landlady (my actual one at that time) has gone insane.

(49)
A handsome young man I know has gone insane. (In fact, he did.)

(50)
The doctor tells me that my heart is diseased, and a friend pays no attention to this.

(51)
A boar, an ancient lizard, and a little donkey live together.

(52)
I am in a rich house. A storm rages outside. A woman has abandoned in the storm a red setter with a tiny pup, another dog, a horse, chickens, a hamster carrying a cedar branch, and Stuart Little (a storybook mouse character) dressed as a soldier. I manage to rescue them all.

(53)
I am living with Pueblo Indians at Zuni or Acoma.

(54)
I am dressed like Joan of Arc, and I am standing between a man and a woman, both kneeling. I give the man a ring, put her hand in his, and touch my sword to the ground between them.

As I record these dreams, they suddenly seem like shattered artifacts found in an excavated ruin—enigmatic in part, identifiable in part because the archeologist is already familiar with the culture even if not with this site, and exciting as I expect all digs are to the involved digger. (Jung, as I recall, said that early in his life he had wanted to be an archeologist.)

As I sort these isolated dreams I recognize the themes, old and new. First comes the feminine dimension in many costumes—analyst, queen, insane landlady, insane acquaintance, the woman who abandons animals, the great rooted pueblo, Joan of Arc, and the bride.

The masculine dimension appears as insane young man, physician, the groom in the marriage rite. The animal archetypes abound: boar, lizard, donkey, dogs, horse, chickens, a hamster and the mouse Stuart Little.

On the whole, the feminine is more discrete, with more dimensions. The queen (45) is secure, courageous, and ready to rule her kingdom. That Miss Wolff was there bridges the space between my Zurich analysis and the other patterns of work and problems. How fortunate that the queen was so strong and far-seeing, because the other feminine dimension persons were not at all what I would have chosen. There is much too much lostness and insanity. My dream ship's crossing (46) was blanketed with lostness and loneliness; the rich woman (52) abandoned the animals; the feelings (the heart in (50)) are not in good shape, and the healer knows this but the friend does not heed it. (I went into the hospital again that year.)

Animals have always been my most numerous dream figures— because I love them, because they are the instinctual side that I have tended to override with my head, and because they are so unbeatably themselves. The boar, the ancient lizard, and the donkey as housemates (51) is sheer foolishness and therefore sheer truthful delight. The Fool is always true and a truth. Equally foolish is a hamster carrying a cedar branch (one of the recurring symbols). And Stuart Little (the mouse) dressed as a soldier (52). But the Fool is the rescuer and healer—as in *The Greater Trumps,* by Charles Williams, where disaster or its opposite depends on the movements of the Fool in the Tarot cards.

Throughout this difficult year of return, readjustment, and new challenges, I needed the Fool.

V

Interim
(1950–1954)

The years beginning with 1950 and ending with 1960 altered my world extensively. However, 1950 to 1954 was an interim period of intense and needed learning of many kinds.

A small group of us, including my two friends who had conducted seminars in southern California with me, decided to make our seminar work into a nonprofit, educational corporation and to eventually move all of it to northern California because of a growing demand for psychological and religious seminars. So the Guild for Psychological Studies, Inc., was formed. The move to the north did not take place until 1956, but the demand for seminars continued, and we began to contemplate training new leaders.

About this time we were forced into a final separation from the Jungian Society in San Francisco. This had been a long time brewing and we had discussed it with psychological and medical professional friends outside of the Society before the final break came. We had been "training" with members of the Society—as it had only recently separated from the Analytical Psychology

Club and was just beginning training—and then the Society
objected to what we were doing in our seminars. They said that
we were putting too much emphasis on the "religious" and that
we were doing "group therapy"—which in fact we have never
done. Dr. Jung himself was as deeply concerned as we were with
the religious problems of our time, and Mrs. Jung became an
honorary sponsor of the Guild for Psychological Studies shortly
before her death in November of 1955. We had been good friends
with many of the Society members and had worked analytically
with some of them. For me at a personal level it increased the
loneliness with which I constantly had to deal. But also it forced
us to come out courageously for what we believed and forced
me to stand on my own convictions.

One unforgettable dream near the beginning of 1950 stood
laughingly beside me for a long time, giving me that support and
comfort that the Fool gives—nonsupport and noncomfort which
is nonetheless comforting because it is so absurdly and ridicu-
lously human:

(55)
*I am playing the role of Hamlet, and at the end of a very drama-
tic scene I fall on my sword and die. Later, after much hue and
cry in the play, I find I am alive and not Hamlet at all but just
a person who needs to live.*

Also I seemed to have more and more dreams about increasing
numbers of nonhuman creatures. One example:

(56)
*I go out into a garden with trees and flowers. It is spring. I see
a mother nuthatch, masked like the American ones but also
resembling the Swiss klieber. A father bird is there too, and they
have a baby between them. I exclaim in joy. Then a cat comes.
Then a dog. I chase the dog, and hold the cat, and then try to
drive it away. Someone finds other young birds—like owls—
under something. Then I see a hawk sweep down and capture
a lovely bluebird. I see a young kitten drowning. Then the
mother nuthatch lights on my head. Slowly and gladly I stand
and offer her some bread. She eats. Then I walk with her toward
the wall of a house. We arrive and I climb up under the chim-*

ney. She folds back the chimney by removing some bricks and
shows me where her babies are safe. Also she says the bread I
have brought is not very nourishing, and I promise to get some
whole grain bread. Then I go to bed outdoors, and I feel that
all small creatures are climbing in with me, and I waken myself
in some anxiety because there are so very many.

The second dream is a far cry from the Hamlet scene—in which
both the pain and the humor reside in the ego's consciousness.
The complicated animal-bird dream has no Fool humor because
all "lower" creatures are natively Fools; the message is that once
you begin to tend to the instinctual life in the unconscious, be
prepared not only for its wisdom but also for its incredible multiplicity! What the ego has to remain aware of is precisely that
multiplicity. We humans so easily tend to believe that there is
only one right way for things to be, whereas the animal kingdom
doesn't "believe" anything but acts in each situation according
to the reality of that situation. Instinct, like the Fool, acts con-
tingently. Even today, for all my relationship to the Fool, I am
just beginning to understand pure contingency.

Again I consider several dreams, alone or grouped, as they seem
to have been walking around many of the needed attitudes and
actions required at this stage of my journey.

(57)
A friend and I are watching a dance. Eleanor Roosevelt is
dancing. Her hands move like many fluttering birds, as in
modern dance or Oriental dance. She was like a dancing Kali.
Her face seemed to be half searching and half in a mood of
mystical madness.

Eleanor Roosevelt (who said she felt like an ugly duckling in
her youth) and her mystical madness of the Kali dance (57) were
vital statements to me; I was so pedestrian and afraid of such
giving over to feeling moods. That she, of all people, could do it,
helped me to see that something in me could do it too.

(58)
Something about religious signs and hangings needing to be in
gayer colors.

(59)
(Half dream and half semi-waking fantasy) *I am in a large palace*
with others—or perhaps an Indian temple. Each person is to
find an animal. I found for myself a small elephant, about three
feet high, wearing elaborate trappings. I patted him, and
named him Kingsbroke.

Dream (58) added to the message. Brighter colors indeed! This
I needed so desperately. Dream (59) brought me again the elephant, the carrier of the Buddha, the sign of the basic beginning
of the kundalini yoga system related to the body and its solid
support system. Kingsbroke? Royal at least.

(60)
I am in the hospital for some follow-up exams. When I ask the
doctor why, he says he is concerned with my heart and my
breathing. Later on, I am in a place like both a hospital and a
school. Many other women are there also, of many different
ages. All seem to be women who have some profession of impor-
tance and success, and yet all are there to do something new,
different, at which they are not skilled. One has been playing
baseball. A well-known actress is naively eager to continue
doing something totally out of her line. An older woman comes
in, supported by two others. She has cut her finger quite badly.
While another woman bandages it, we all break into a silly
rollicking song. Someone says, "That was a cheerful accident."
The most important thing was that every woman was trying
something at which she was not skilled, some new thing.

(61)
I am with several other women. A voice says, "Stand up and be
counted." It is as if to do so meant to be part of a courageous
minority affirming something.

Dreams (60) and (61) are both concerned with the feminine
dimension and its healing, which comes about through doing the
unusual and the awkward things, enjoying doing them even if
mistakes are made, and affirming yourself as a minority.

(62)
I am looking for some important item of my own, but realize

I can only find it if I take off my shoes and wade through knee-deep muddy water brought there by a flood.

Dream (62) is a neat, down-to-earth statement about what is needed if one is to find one's own. It is to descend into the mud and the flood and wade with great difficulty through it. It harks back to one of the earliest dreams (3) which told me at the almost-beginning how it would always be.

When I had time I continued my personal analysis—but it was sparse. I never failed to record the messages from the inner dreamer. And there were certain definite trends in my dream world.

For example, there were seven very important dreams having to do with notable people such as the Jungs, the Sitwells, the Roosevelts, the British royal family. There were several dreams of air and sky happenings, and two outstandingly important religious ones. Animal dreams continued to multiply. Art forms and ancient artifacts appeared in quite a few. Many, many dreams related to various aspects of the feminine dimension. These were the primary stresses of my inner journey and my inner dreamer.

(63)
Two women are standing silhouetted against the sky. One is dressed in a long cape like Edith Sitwell wore—but this one is dark green with gold trim. She is looking beyond to some unseen place. The second woman kneels near her, and is working at unraveling threads which they will follow to some treasure. It must be done slowly. I know that both women are me.

(64)
I see a large castle, composed of four spherical, or egg-shaped, parts. It is a place where one goes to rest, introvert, revalue. Each egg-shaped part has a separate meaning. The castle is in a remote location.

(65)
I am going in a donkey cart up a mountain, perhaps in Italy, as the road is narrow and old, as if it were a Roman stone path overgrown with dark green here and there. It drops off steeply on the right. A small boy, 5 or 6, is in the cart on my right, and

my arm is around him protectively. And from somewhere a dog comes and climbs in on my right, and sits very close. I am watching out for her as well. I know we will have to go through difficult places, and the donkey is a very small one. But it continues through all obstacles as we proceed slowly.

Dreams (63), (64) and (65) showed the stress of slow and patient work. Each is concerned with "slow unraveling," or "rest" in the egg-shaped castle, or the small, slow, patient donkey, or helping the little boy home. Patience, despite my being a "sensation type," sometimes is hard to come by. I can be exceedingly angry *inside* when something goes wrong that I have tried to do right, or when someone who is all thumbs tries to make something work. Worst of all was my total and derisive impatience with myself for any mistake at all.

The second major theme relates to the religious and aesthetic nature of the feminine dimension as it now begins to appear. Dream (63) is very important for this reason. The "I" of me, the ego personality, is here *both* as the poet in royal earth colors *and also* the prosaic unraveler of those threads leading to the treasure. I had recently been at a poetry reading by Dame Edith Sitwell.

Dame Sitwell emerged during World War II as a poet of emotional depth and profoundly human concerns. She was equally famed for her formidable personality, Elizabethan dress and eccentric opinions. She entered walking slowly down the aisle, gowned in medieval robes, took her place on the platform with great dignity and with equal dignity drew from a large black bag she carried both her books and a large handkerchief with which she lustily blew her nose. To me this was unbelievably magnificent to be able to do. She was herself. She walked as herself, blew her nose as herself, read her poems wonderfully as herself. Her poems explored the musical quality of words and religious symbolism. A few nights later in a dining car en route to Los Angeles, I saw her and sent a note of gratitude for the reading; she sent me in return a delightful reply. Her quality of self-ness worked directly into my psyche and told me that such selfness might become a part of me. But also I needed the kneeling un-raveler, the slow work to eventually find the treasure.

Dream (64) carries the feminine dimension theme forward. The egg-shaped parts of the castle each resembled the Cosmic Egg of the Orphic Mysteries, where the egg is the world germ or the womb of the future. There are four of these womb-stages, each having a different meaning not stated in the dream. The castle, made of the four egg-shaped parts, is for introversion, inwardness, finding new values in a deeply feminine dimension way.

(66)
I'm on a voyage on a great ship. Another ship comes near to us. It is very unusual, having been built for a special group called the Valaisians. They are religious actors. At one point I am in the corridor of their ship which is rich with drapes and has gilt ceilings as in a baroque church. A long line of these actors carrying huge sheafs of lilac blossoms come to greet all the ships and people as they land at Le Havre.

(67)
I see a huge elephant coming toward me. I hold onto his ear, I think. Anyway, I am carried along, riding slowly and safely high up by his head. I know I am safe, and feel very secure.

I feel that the Valaisians in dream (66) are welcomers, are carriers of spring blossoms, are people from the earthy mountain region of Switzerland, and also are feminine folk figures of joy, grace, and of the sea. The sea, ships and storms and sea-mammals have continued to be central symbols to me through the years.

(68)
An Indian medicine man is initiating me into some Mayan or Aztec mysteries. The crucial moment is when he leads me out into the light. He stands behind me and lifts my skirt so that the sun can fall directly on my genitals. Although I am embar-rassed, he is quite objective and detached, turning me so the sun comes from just the right direction. As the sun's rays hit my body, the feeling is orgiastic and exciting.

Dream (68) is without doubt an initiation ritual for the young feminine. Factually, one of the scenes in the Navajo Emergence Myth is the impregnating of Changing Woman, the highest deity, by a drop of water and a shaft of sunlight. Not only my conscious but my unconscious knew this scene, chose to put it into a Mayan or Aztec setting, and added the very important medicine man. Spirit and substance are brought together in this psychological/ religious puberty ceremony. It is possible, it is to be hoped for, that the "I" of me was beginning to come of age in its journey toward the Self of me. So much more than that. So very much more.

The following dream had to be the last of the Milestones because in it, for the first time, I consciously placed myself in the moving stream of Time, Time the Mother, the Grandmother, the Earth and all its changes and flowings. She was the gypsy that I felt my mother to be. She was related to the very early waking dream I had of a little old gnomish man who came to me and said, "Why don't you listen to Gypsy music?" She was Changing Woman, the ancient feminine who continually dies and is renewed. She belonged to the Child as well as to Death. She was mine as well as the world's.

(69)

I am talking with a male classmate—one who is near my age and I like him—saying that I have had a very important dream and want to share it. He is agreeable, although he leaves the room and returns a couple of times. The last page of the dream has a poem I have written about some deep aspect of the spirit. I have recorded the dream, with each page having a dream object on it. The last page has the poem, with vines traced across it, and on it also an actual leaf, very ancient and fragile. I tease it loose gently and on the back of it is an ancient inscription, almost illegible.

(70)

A voice choir has been planned for reading a poem, but nobody's voice is strong enough to lead off but mine. So I improvise a poem about an old relief carving I am holding. It portrays the Nativity scene. I recall seeing and making words about Virgin, and Mother, a wreath and the Child.

Both dreams (69) and (70) concern the deeper mysteries of the archetypes of the spirit. Both have in them poems. The most intimate and richest expression of my journey is when a poem comes right. The ancient vine, the ancient leaf with its very ancient inscription—these are mysteries going back to Dionysus, a god of ecstasy. Which is what poetry is in the soul's house. The symbols in (70) are very feminine ones—Virgin, Mother, Wreath (or Circle), Child.

(71)
I am in a wooded place where I see a young boy wandering through the trees searching for his grandmother. I join him and seem to be helping him. At last we see her, a little, bent old woman, her hair awry, one foot lame. She is hunting for a place to die, I think. She goes along testing each tree, poking her cane into the trees as if to find a hollow into which she can crawl. We watch from a distance. Then she goes into a little store in the woods. In the store are many children and a few adults. She is behind the counter. The children laugh at her and I feel angry with them. But she only smiles and starts to sing some old and slightly ribald folksong. Slowly the children all join in, until all are singing and responding to her free, natural, moving quality. Suddenly I realize she is an old gypsy. The young boy and I move toward her, singing. I feel she is my grandmother too. Our faces slowly get closer to hers, and while we still sing, each of us, at her gesture, kisses one of her cheeks very gently. Then I am crying, tears that I cannot stop pouring down my cheeks. I see others are crying also. I take one of her fragile and withered old hands, kiss it, and say to her, between tears and joy, that if only I can be as wonderful as her when I grow older I will be satisfied.

This final dream is a part of this Interim section. It belongs here because it seems to be a link between several periods: the period before 1955 and my work with Mrs. Jung and Dr. Adler and after; the period before 1955 and my Ph.D. and full professional status and after; the period before my seeing Jordan and Israel and all the places that I had only read about and imagined and wondered

about and the seeing of which finally enabled me to complete
Joseph's Son (which remains my most loved book of all I have
written) and after. *After* all these events I was changed, grown,
altered, different.

VI

Many Milestones
(1955–1959)

(72)
Just a sense, on waking, that one way to cope with anxiety is related to the words, "Before the world was, I am."

This dream prefaced a summer of seminars just preceding a second trip to Europe. It deepened my belief that I can cope with anxiety by seeing things in a different perspective, by continually putting myself in the framework of eternity, of that which exists before the world, or my life. It seemed to me then that these words when they were first phrased, and when they came to me in my dream, were the ultimate statement of the nature of God, of that evolutionary Force moving behind and beyond time and change and death and life.

In my life I have searched for the relation of the individual spirit to the God Presence, for religious meanings, from the first. My Christmas day birthday was important to me from my early years. Shortly after learning to talk I informed my family that they each had names; my father was named Jesus, my mother was St. Cecilia, my brother was an Indian, and I was DeeDee (my nickname for myself).

I left the church of my childhood when I was about sixteen. The baptism and confirmation in my early twenties in the Anglican church was one of my first major choices. After I drifted away from the church, I nonetheless was concerned with religious practices, studied the western mystics, and even did some work in meditation with one of the leading Hindu swamis.

I found my richest religious meanings after I began attending seminars on the life and teachings of Jesus, and began to see how they related to the psychologies of Kunkel and Jung.

All this recapitulation of the spiritual dimensions of my life is by way of saying that these Milestone years—including two trips to Zurich and deep analysis—were extensions of the spirit in essential ways. This period began in Zurich in 1955 on Twelfth Night. My friends and I had just arrived and been greeted in the *pension* by a candle-lighted tree and an old phonograph playing Christmas carols. It was good to be back again.

Mrs. Emma Jung was one of the most interesting people I have ever known. What a gift it was to work with her analytically. She was warm, quiet, penetrating of insight, had a sense of humor, and always confronted in the most direct way. I saw her in the Jung home in Kusnacht outside Zurich, which meant that several times a week I rode the Swiss train from Zurich to Kusnacht, watched the lake and its daily moods, and sat in a tearoom, if there was snow on the ground, until it was time for my hour.

Emma Jung was an absolutely marvelous and beautiful woman. She had a kind of courage and genuineness that very few people have. Though she always gave the impression of a typical German *hausfrau* relating to all her household help and the children, she was so far from it. She had a point of view quite her own, and what she felt, she said.

She had a wisdom and depth and I admired her courage. After she had raised her children she studied different languages, became a therapist, wrote a wonderful book on the Parsifal legend and moreover was a definite human being who led a full life.

These dreams were worked on in my first hour with Mrs. Jung:

(73)
*I waken in my cabin at night. My little black dog is asleep on
the floor and she is bathed in and surrounded by a glowing
light. I am afraid and awed, wondering what is the source of
this mysterious light. I get up and look out my cabin window.
A very near, luminous, larger than life-size, full moon is in the
sky, and its light covers the dog. Awesomely on the face of the
full moon, sharp in clear black, is the sign of Capricorn.*

(74)
*A huge spider is trying to strangle a faery with its web. I get
hold of the web's strand and try desperately to break it, or to
saw it through on some sharp surface. I cannot. The faery is
being slowly choked to death. Finally I find a large kitchen knife
and saw the strand. Later on I see Oberon and Titania. I am
wearing a white jeweled cape and am somehow related to the
faeries.*

(75)
*I am on a small cruise ship where first class is empty and those
in the lower class are having all the fun. We are en route to a
Mardi Gras. Then I am in some Swiss village where they are
celebrating Twelfth Night. Some people are quite drunk and not
honoring the festival. I am watching the ritual. Someone says
that there are two sorts of people—those who lose sight of the
real values and those who do not. I see a group of women
participants all wearing witches' hats, domino masks, and
carrying lanterns. They are acting out the role of Befana, the
good witch who brings gifts on Twelfth Night. (This was the
night of our arrival in Zurich, in actual fact.)*

Dream (73) led eventually to my experience with astrology. It
brought to my attention what Neumann calls the "matriarchal
consciousness" which he related to the moon. The moon spirit
comes to fruition in darkness secretly from the head ego—"a
mysterioum in a mysterium." In old times, Mrs. Jung said, candles
were lighted on trees in the wood as offerings to the nature spirit.
The moon is the "divine feminine archetype," she said, and then
suggested, relative to the Capricorn symbol, that I have my horoscope done.

When we talked about dreams (74) and (75) Mrs. Jung said,

"You must be related to the faery world, to early European
pagan cults. These symbols are compensatory to Christian consciousness." That is precisely why Christian Science was damag-
ing to me, because all the darkness of substance was denied, and
why I was drawn to Jesus, who was not a carrier of Christian
consciousness.

I had seen my mother as being related to witches and faeries
(as I feel she was in her own unconscious) and because I could not
be like her, I lost my own unique connections with this faery
world and lived out her other side. The first indication of this
(although not at all clear to me for a long time) had appeared in
the first two dreams I had recorded, the Terrible Dream(s) about
being in hell and belonging to the devil and then about flying off
into the night sky with a sort of batlike masculine being.

Dream (74) said what must be done now—to cut away the
"mother" web and free the faery, to find Oberon and Titania
and my place with relationship to them. Dream (75) said more of
the same but differently—differentiating between unconsciousness, drunkenness, etc., and a conscious relationship to the dark
witch mother, Befana the gift-bringer.

After we had talked about dream (73), Mrs. Jung asked, "Why
don't you have my daughter do your horoscope?"

This question was as startling to me—or almost—as the first
time I was asked to consider seeing the graphologist, or the first
time I thought about seeing the hand analyst. These things challenged to the roots my deeply ingrained rational side, although
this time less so. By now I had seen the merits of adding such
insights to analysis and spiritual practices—but not, I must add,
as practiced by far too many "astrologists," "graphologists,"
and "chirologists" who have no depth dimension of training and
insight and no knowledge of the depths of the human soul.

My confidence in Mrs. Jung was such that I already had confidence in her daughter, Gret Bauman. Mrs. Jung said that she did
not tell her daughter anything about the person she was sending
except nationality, sex, age, and that they were working with
her. So I went. Once again I was astounded by the incredible
accuracy and truth of the horoscope when handled with religious

concern. Here is a sample of what it said:

Many opposites appear which are extreme in nature, with many difficult aspects. There is a strong creative and intuitive element, but it is very hard to keep it from being swept away by the dark and irrational forces. There is much movement in the unconscious, often unclear or even irritating to the clear and precise conscious life . . . There is seriousness, ambition, goal-directedness. The very difficult aspects make for drive and extreme efforts of will . . . The planet of one's ideals is in the house of death and rebirth. This means that one must work deeply with the unconscious . . . The great oppositions between planets mean that relating to reality is hard . . . There can be many hauntings from a "ghostly" world, hard to deal with . . .

There is an imperative need to go the individual way and a good feel for it . . . Probably the early feminine elements had to be sacrificed, and have now to be refound. The Sun was chosen in the first half of life—perhaps due to the mother—and now the Moon must be chosen . . .

Most of your signs are introverted but to be too much alone is dangerous . . . Things do not come easily in any way . . . A strong artistic gift, and it must be used . . . You are well related to the collective unconscious, but it is harder to get at the personal unconscious elements . . .

Feelings were enclosed, held back, sacrificed, early in life. The mother was problem, as well as the inner irrational forces. Thus the Moon and feelings sacrificed in the first half of life. Your real profession has only come in the second half of life through work with dreams and the unconscious . . . There is a great emphasis on religion—but in a large sense, very new and unorthodox . . . An ideal relationship to the profession you choose, with the feminine side related to it . . . There are bound to be good and faithful friendships, with real personalities, never superficial ones.

The insight about the extreme nature of the opposites in my horoscope helps me always to remember that they are there, pulling against each other. I must remember this and have patience with myself when I seem not to be functioning as I wish

I were, and I must wait until my feelings are ready to surface and then help them as one helps a child to be born. That I have had to work deeply with the unconscious is surely an essential truth. It comes at me from the depths and intends to be heard. I have neither had nor ever wanted a great many friends. The few that I have, and have had, are certainly not superficial but real people concerned with both the inner and the outer worlds.

I have had my horoscope "progressed" many times by her, and find that it inevitably speaks clearly to where I am and to what I need.

(76)
I am at some resort and am to introduce my father to some woman. But when I do so, I say, first, "This is the one who comes from the laundry." Then I say, "This is Sheila's father." I introduce myself, shaking the woman's hand.

This dream, coming very early in my work with Mrs. Jung, was a real shocker. I was totally bewildered as to what it might mean, although I did all I could with it alone. In the next session of analysis, Mrs. Jung suggested that perhaps she was the unknown woman and my very strange introduction meant we had to "clean up" some problem about my father. Where we ultimately came out was a very freeing place.

It was as if I had been caught between my mother's unlived life and my father's nonfulfilment of her need for masculine strength, intellectual power, and success. (My father, bless him, was none of these. He was gentle, loving, nonintellectual, physically an athlete in his youth, and not a success in the world.) So I took on the role of what he might have been had he carried her ideal of a man in Jungian terms, her animus. Their marriage was archetypal and unconscious, more unique than most because both of them were engaged to others when they met, they eloped on Hallowe'en, and they had been married for nearly forty years when my mother died. I lived out whatever was unconscious from the level of primitive archetypes. Also Mrs. Jung pointed out, with a father whose feminine dimension was contained in the "mother-daughter" I would have had to get involved with older men—as with the Anglican priest who helped me, and as with Harry. This dream strongly warned me *not* to be the "laundryman" for other people's dirty clothes, *not* to get caught in playing the "masculine father" role—strong, helpful, rational, etc.

Then came a dream which opened up another sort of insight about the spirit and sent me into a long active imagination fantasy, and into the use of fantasy in fiction writing.

(77)

I have returned from being away. (Both where I had been and where I returned to were unknown places.) My animals are back with me. There are two lizards as large as baby alligators. The older one I hold in my arms, the other I lead like a dog on a leash. The one I hold is very very old and wrinkled. I say to him, "Hello, Oh Ancient of Days." The other is playfully nipping at my feet as a glad puppy will, and I tell him not to be jealous. I also have a tiny kitten and other more usual animals.

This dream opened up the deep realm of ancient chthonic wisdom, archaic, not yet conscious, but benign. The younger lizard was a new power preparing for maturation. The scene was like a great alchemical description. I read and reread the descriptions from the Book of Daniel in the Old Testament and realized that the Ancient of Days was a vision of God for Daniel. I took the dream into an active imagination (written and unplanned fantasy):

First I put the Old One (the Ancient of Days) on the ground. He did not want to move, so all of us just stood there quietly . . . [Some days later I continued.] The Old One moved ponderously toward a body of water like a lake. He seemed about to go in. The Young One moved faster, up a beach to my left. Both seemed to want me to follow and I was torn between them so didn't go in any direction. [Later I incorporated a current dream about a beach with very high waves.] I wondered if the Old One was going into these waves. The Young One still waited for me. Then I saw a huge fire, with some orgiastic scene on the beach. I joined in for a time, being passionately embraced by a strange and primitive man. Meanwhile the Young One

was still waiting, and the Old One seemed to resemble an Old
Man of the Sea, half fish, moving into the waves. [Some days
later I continued.] I saw the Old One seated on a throne, but
looking not only like a great lizard but also like a very archaic
Mother-Goddess. And the Young One was a red lizard or salamander on the Old One's lap as the Son of man.

The active imagination opened up a new dimension of the
uroboric world of the great, timeless unconscious populated with
undifferentiated beings "in the beginning of things." The movement was toward greater differentiation. The salamander is of
water and earth. In alchemy, it can survive the fire as an archaic
form of the spirit needing to evolve. The fact that the Old One
became a Mother-Goddess was a further expression of my deep
relationship to the feminine aspect of the Other—which had
begun with my feelings for the European Black Virgin figures.

The red salamander as the Son of man was most startling—
and yet it made sense to me. Jesus' use of the phrase "Son of
man" made it very close to the concept of the Self—not at all
as referring to himself or to any apocalyptically cosmic judge.
This fitted in with the commonplace little salamander seated on
the Mother-Goddess's lap. Today as always it is most important
for me to keep my Human-Being-Self always related somehow to
the Mother-Goddess—to the Feminine Godhead—lest I lose my
way among the omnipresent pressures and demands of the outer
world. She is vital to me, and She needs to be more vital to the
planet and its people if we are to survive.

Also in this period I had a dream about my friend who was
dying. She had shared an apartment with me after I left home.
This truly marked the end of an era of my life—an era of protest,
revolt, and confusion. I also had several dreams of various aspects
of the Fool—people dressed in motley, Jung writing a book on
Chagall. Here is one of them.

(78)
I am in a Swiss village trying to find the railway station. It is
night. I am aware of, or talking to someone about, how hard
it is to adjust to new names and a new language. Then I see a

*big show being staged in a huge theater on many levels. I am
to be part of some planned act. But shortly before time for us
to go on, things go wrong, with some not there, costumes mis-
laid, etc. The time draws closer and I feel desperate. Finally
I say I will just have to go on and ad lib. I ask people to get
me some clothes—old baggy pants, an old shirt, coat, and
knitted cap. I tell the stage manager to turn up the lights until
I am in the center of the main stage. Then I shuffle on stage,
just letting myself be natural and responding to whatever is at
hand. At each level of the stage I react to different things and
people. One level has stacks of mattresses on which I step and
they topple me over. The situations are funny-poignant—as
with a Charlie Chaplin type of clown. Friends are here and
there, and members of my family. I throw myself deeply into the
part, give as fully and freely as I can. When I finish I am ex-
hausted. But to my amazement people come to me—friends,
family, strangers—to tell me what a fine thing I have done.
At first I cannot believe this. Then I do, and wonder how I
am to use this gift in the future.*

This was really the full acceptance of my own humanity—
because above all else the true Fool is humanness and fallibility
and erring. I needed this side of humanness to come forward as
a balance to my pedantic, rational, unrelated side.

An excerpt from my journal shows the conscious dealing with
this theme:

> When the Clown moves too fast, or too aggressively, he falls
> over his own feet and becomes ludicrous—and precisely this is
> his pathos. My head-ego must be suspended, so that the heart
> ego can tell me where I am. The phrases "Before the world was,
> I am," and "Hello, Oh Ancient of Days," now say to me that
> the world of timelessness is where I need to live for awhile, I who
> have been so driven by time.

(79)
*I am at Einsiedeln, or some other place like it, with a Black
Virgin. Someone is saying that this mystery or spirit cannot be
understood by everyone, which is why such places are remote.*

(80)

Discussing with Mrs. Jung the fact that every Swiss city (and European city) has its own spirit which is related to it. We particularly mention Basel and Lucerne—and one city which has a spirit of a woman riding on some beast of burden. I seem to see her on either a horse or a camel.

(81)

Walking in a Swiss city or village where there is some miraculous religious image. We must go underground in a passage to reach it. Someone shows us (gives us?) a very lovely object like a baptismal font, although this can be used in one's own room because it can be put into the wash bowl. It is shaped like a flower cup with an open end. It is of soft cream-colored pottery with blue-violet overtones.

These three dreams all concern the Feminine Spirit in some way: the remoteness of access of the Black Virgin, the spirit of the Woman riding on the beast of burden. All of them emphasize the chthonic forces of the Spirit and point to the need to go to a deep earth-layer of Being, "deeper than the stream of the unconscious in order to contact and understand the creative spirit of Darkness," said Mrs. Jung. The washbowl baptismal font was related to finding a personal individual baptism into a new way— one that draws its living water from the bottom upward. The color of the font in the dream resembled a painting I had done of barren waiting earth and a grey-blue sky.

(82)

I am sitting near Linda Fierz in her bed, talking with her about the creation myths.

(83)

I waken with the words "In the beginning, in the small and the great darkness."

Dreams (82) and (83) refer to one of the most important people in my life. I had studied with her personally in the field of comparative mythology, and she considered me as close as a daughter. She gave to me richly of her wisdom. She died of cancer soon after I left Zurich.

I had seen Linda Fierz at the hospital, sat beside her bed, talked with her about myths (at her insistence) because she had certain things about death which she wanted to say. She had deepened my knowledge of comparative mythology as no other person ever did.

I talked about all these things with Mrs. Jung and told her I wanted to write a book on Navajo mythology, especially the Creation story—which Mrs. Fierz and I had worked on. I wanted to carry on some of her deep and poetic contributions. Mrs. Jung felt that this was very right, both as a tribute and as a carrying forward of some of Mrs. Fierz's insights. Dream (83) gave to me the words with which I in fact began the book, *A Magic Dwells,* which is dedicated to her.

Among the last dreams I worked on with Mrs. Jung before my departure from Switzerland (and Mrs. Jung's death, also from cancer) were these:

(84)
In a small Swiss alpine village. I go into a shop to buy food and wine. Mrs. Jung is there also. I ask for rotesweine, but am given a special delicate white wine.

(85)
In a small village high in the alps of the Tessin. It is the time of a feast day for the village saint, a woman. A village woman is telling me about it.

My own relationship both to Mrs. Jung as rooted feminine being and to the Swiss villages was clear in dreams (84) and (85). Villages like these are an intrinsic part of the earth and the mountains on which they stand. Despite the building of them with the stones of the earth by the hands of men, they remain deeply feminine. Each village in the Tessin—the Italian part of Switzerland—does have its feast day for its patron saint. Mine seemed to be feminine:

(86)
In a lovely European city with snow deep on the ground, streets very steep and cobbled, and I wonder how I will be able to get to the cathedral. It is a particularly beautiful one, resembling

*the Freiburg cathedral. I wonder why someone doesn't clear
the streets, then I realize this is a completely cooperative com-
munity, and that every member of it will contribute to the
snow-clearance.*

(87)
*In a European village where there has been a great flood. The
waters have receded and it is found that the figure of the Virgin
has remained untouched by the waters except for the hem of
Her robe.*

Dreams (86) and (87) were clear statements of aspects of the
Feminine spiritual dimensions. Gothic cathedrals lift and soar,
but they are nonetheless fastened to earth by gargoyles and other
creatures, as well as by multiform plants and animals carved in
the stone. Two remarkable things about dream (87) were that the
Virgin was not harmed by the floods and that once again the mysterious "knowing" of my unconscious was revealed. I learned
from Mrs. Jung *after* the dream that old legends say that mer-
maids who become human keep their relationship to the water
world by having wet hems to their skirts, that there is a village in
Switzerland with a legend about the Virgin having survived a
flood with only her skirt wet, and that the Virgin as Stella Maris
is both Queen of Heaven and Mother of Nature.

The last dream (88) I did with Mrs. Jung before leaving Switzerland (and she died that year) was a true milestone in many ways.
I dreamt it the night before I saw her for that last hour—and on
the night before I had my second and last individual hour with
Dr. Jung. All of these events took place at Ascona, on the Italian
lakes where the Jungs were spending a few weeks.

(88)
*I am in a large town square where many people are gathering
for a conference. They are Jungians all, including Dr. and Mrs.
Jung. They are all having their pictures taken, and I realize
I have gotten too close and must lie flat so as not to get in the
pictures. Then I walk away from the group and a young woman
asks if my friend and I are going to be leaders for some Jungian
conference next year. I say no, that we will just be present. She*

says, "You will be more than just present." Then I see Dr. Jung
walking in my direction, and feel I must speak to him even
though he will not know me. He is very tall, and I lean back to
look at him. He looks down with a smile, and puts his arm
about me as a father would and greets me. I say how happy I
am to see him again and he seems pleased. Then someone asks
him about the difference between God and the unconscious and
he laughs, then says very seriously, "Don't worry about that yet.
Wait until Aquarius comes in." Then I am in a small anteroom
with stone floors just outside where the Jungians are meeting in
a large hall. I hear a faint sound like an animal crying, as if
trapped. There is no place for it to be. I feel it must be caught
under a chest of drawers on the only piece of ground not cov-
ered by the stone floor. I tip the chest over. Under it is a horrible
mess of vomit and dirt and I see something in this mess. I look
closer. Slowly I go near, making myself look. I see a tiny baby,
lovely in the face, covered with vomit. I think it is dead—but
I see it is breathing. I rush into the big room where the meeting
is going on and say that I want a nurse and a doctor immed-
iately. I hope they will be able to save the baby.

This dream sharply delineated the problems with the orthodox
Jungian group which I described earlier. Mrs. Jung felt that I was
here being too self-effacing and fearful, not daring to take a
chance on my own ideas and feelings and their worth. She felt
that the girl's words underlined the fact that I (we) did have a
place in Jungian thought, more than "just being present." The
scene with Dr. Jung affirmed that I was not only related well to
Jungian ideas but that my relationship was sound and good, that
I belonged, that I was connected to the "spiritual father." The
reference to the Aquarian Age—which I had never thought much
about and did not yet understand—indicated that perhaps neither
I nor the culture can see the meaning of the difference between
the deep unconscious archetypes and the ineffable Mystery
behind them except by being aware that a new thing is coming.

This new age of the Anthropos has to do with personal individuation, maybe a new kind of religious approach which we cannot
yet describe. The anteroom related to the mystery initiations, as
at Villa de Misteri at Pompeii, and to being at the threshhold of

one's own true being. At this threshold was the animal nature
crying out, almost dead from neglect and needing desperately
to be rescued. That it was a human baby, and that my concern
was like that of a distraught mother, made it the feeling side at a
human rather than animal level. The mess it lay in resembled the
prima materia of alchemy in which the Self is found. Alchemical
texts often show it as revolting, repulsive, ugly, inferior, and
yet as containing the new life. Getting a doctor and nurse is
entering into the inner chamber, not intellectually but with a
demand for my own feeling needs. "This," said Mrs. Jung, "is
how you must now come into your new creativity."

During this and my previous trips to Zurich I had been privil-
eged to spend many hours with Dr. Jung and at times with Mrs.
Jung, either in their garden at their Kusnacht home or taking
walks in the countryside. Ascona was one such time and the last
time I was to see the Jungs. Dr. Jung and I were walking by the
lake and we were talking about myths—more precisely about
the inner myth and what happens inside us. I asked if the inner
myth was an aspect of God, and he said that all inner myths
related to God—that it all belonged, in one sense, to the larger
being. The Self beyond the Self so to speak.

I always felt that there was no question as to where Dr. Jung
or Mrs. Jung stood in regard to the religious feeling they both
carried and of what was really happening and/ or what needed
to happen in the psyche.

The day they posed for the picture outside the Hotel in Ascona,
Dr. Jung and I had just returned from a walk and I offered to go in
and get Mrs. Jung as they were about to go out. He waved his cane
at me, as if to say it was his to do and said to me in a wonderfully
cavalier fashion "*I* shall go get my wife."

My horoscope had already shown how intellect and reason
and work had to dominate the first part of my life so that irrational forces would not sweep me away. But now the feminine
spiritual feelings for the inner world must become dominant.
Maybe, I said, I needed to write and see if the words could begin
to flow. If they did, or if they didn't, I would learn to see the difference between procrastinating and waiting.

X.   C. G. and Emma Jung, Ascona, 1955

XI.   Linda Fierz, around 1955

To end on this theme was immeasurably important—especially because I later had to face the fact of Mrs. Jung's death. The dream of the next night gave me much to work with:

(89)
I was telling some young women (some of them patients) about why they needed to trust the growth process no matter how hard it was. I told them how Dr. Jung had said that everyone comes for help feeling that his or her problem is unique, that the hole belonging to each one is the deepest and worst—and how Jung said then that the myth helps each one to see that humankind for thousands of years has known about holes and has known also that there was always a way to get out of holes.

Mrs. Jung phoned me to tell me of Linda Fierz's surgery and its doubtless outcome. And later Mrs. Jung wrote to me telling me of Linda's death. Her thoughtfulness and wisdom touched me deeply.

We had a wonderful and leisurely time exploring Italy from Rome to Naples and south, then back up the Italian coast. Finally we spent some time in England where I had a few sessions with Dr. Barker, a warm, tweedy Britisher much in touch with his feminine dimension although craggy and male. His concern for what he called "the dawn child" in every person helped my transition back to America, including my incorporating the death of Mrs. Fierz.

Coming home was coming into seminars and a search for a new center for our seminars, and above all coming into the knowledge, sudden and shocking, that a dear man friend, Mark Pelgrin, was stricken with cancer. Many of my dreams after leaving Switzerland prepared me for what lay ahead. I relate only a few.

(90)
I am searching for some fabled golden figures of a man and a woman. Then I see them, as if at a great distance, twined about a very large hand—and I know it is the Hand of God.

(91)
With friends in an Italian city. The main square, in the very

center of the city, is a four-fold mandala.

(92)
I see a large, two-wheeled cart drawn by a small donkey—like some in Italy. Some important event is about to happen. Then I see that on the cart are seated Mrs. Jung and two or three little children. She waves at us, smiling maternally.

(93)
Some others and I are to have a meal. The food that is brought in is fish cakes. They are on plates, sliced, looking exactly like the sacred bread in the Villa de Misteri scene. Also, they are vari-colored, like the marble in Florentine buildings, and also like the robe of the Virgin of Peace in one of the great Florentine paintings. (Angelico?)

(94)
There is an animal (dog or large cat?) which is somehow also partly a feminine human being. But both parts are alive and well because periodically the head is placed on the body and is fed and both parts are nourished. A male doctor is attending this animal and he tells me to put my hand on the body to see how alive it is. I do, and it is very warm and vibrant. I ask if it can be put together, and he says that of course he is going to sew the head on again and it will be whole.

To be assured that the masculine and the feminine images were both in the Hand of God—to know that the center of the City is a mandala—to know that Mrs. Jung was alive and maternally related to earth and the Child inside me—to be reminded that the unconscious food is related to Florence and the Virgin of Peace—these were the messages that kept me going when all the homecoming stresses and sorrows began to move in, as they always do for everyone after a rich descent into the depths of the spirit.

Our lives are forever human lives. And these inner movements and religious undergirdings are the events that are counterpoises to the daily humanity of existence, nourishing the spiritual life.

Dream (94) warned as well as reassured me about the inner problem of the split between my mind and body. It clearly announced that the task of healing was far from complete, but it also stated that the work was going on, that a healer was at work, that the feminine was vibrantly alive even if still separated from itself. I returned to this dream again and again when the events of outer and inner life seemed almost unendurable and insurmountable.

Many outer events filled the time between June 1955 and December 1959: moving our seminar center from southern to northern California; having many more seminars and giving more seminars in other cities; encompassing the death of the dear male friend (chronicled in *And A Time To Die*); beginning work on *A Magic Dwells* with assistance from a Bollingen Foundation Grant; having a major operation; carrying a heavy analytic practice. The religious search and the inner life continued, of course, but my journals are skimpy for this time as if the outer manifestations of the inner search took precedence, for better or for worse.

The nature of my dreams was mixed. Many dealt with my lostness and confusion in difficult situations. Many dealt with the insanity of others, and death, and accident, and suicide, floods and explosions. On the other hand, there were several outstanding ones of Navajo land and its people and my relationship to them. Several deeply religious messages came through. Here are a few representative dreams.

(95)
I am in Switzerland and enter a room where I find Dr. Jung in bed resting. He is much older but very warm to me. He asks me to rest beside him and talk. I do, and we have a long talk with me feeling like a child cuddled up to a wonderful grandfather. He tells me something about large, earthy stones on which he is carving.

(96)
I am with a woman friend who is dying of cancer. She looks thin and ill. I leave the room briefly, hear someone scream, and rush back to find that another friend has come in and found that the ill one has hanged herself.

Dream (95) goes with the earlier dream about Jung (88), reminding me that the Wise Old Man was still there, and that I could keep my inner Child related to him. The stone carving stressed my need to remember the slow and patient work of creation, which Jung himself had always demonstrated so fully. Dream (96) makes plain the totally opposite possibility—that of running away from the hard demands of the death-rebirth-death cycle. With all the outer stresses I needed to be reminded of this danger over and over.

(97)
I feel I am falling into disaster. I see a scene of the world. A galleon breaks through into outer space through the edge of the world into billowing clouds. I shout out poetry as it falls, describing my doom, as I fall clear out of the world.

(98)
I am in the southwest Navajo country. I see an upthrust of vol-canic rock. I pace it off. I decide a little house can be built there with an upstairs, a skylight in the roof, a spiral stair leading up. The rock is reddish brown. The house will be light inside.

(99)
Several friends and I are facing voluntary death. It was time to die. One just chose to let oneself reverse the life sequence, growing younger and younger to infancy, then to nothingness. I chose, but felt very reluctant, and hoped we would not have to begin soon. I had a sense, not of fear or anxiety, but of inevitability, and of transcience, and of wanting to get as much done as possible first.

Dream (97) is one of the archetypal and catastrophic warnings that always help me remember again the flaws in my nature and the dangerous states into which I can fall unless I am vigilant. And (98), again showing the totally opposite possibility, tells what can happen if I do stay related to the earthy stones and spaces of my native and deeply loved outer and inner country. There I can find a true home. Dream (99) wisely puts together the human sense of limitation of life and the creatively human desire to make the most of that life.

(100)
A voice says, "I suffer thee to go. Come and drink blood from the book."

(101)
A voice says, "Seek ye Him."

(102)
A voice says, "Stop seeking who you are and start asking whom you seek."

These three religious dreams—for when the Voice speaks to me, as far as I am concerned it is always the Voice of the Other—were full of numinosity and mystery. As best I can state it, dream (100) reminds me not to get stuck in a regressive place in myself, but to let myself be pushed by the Voice—which inevitably means that the book of my life is once again opened so that its most living substance may be taken inside.

Dream (101), "Seek ye Him," is related to the Other, the Logos meaning of the Self to be sought and sought with all the strength I have. Dream (102) scarcely needs further elucidation. How clear can the inner dreamer be in telling us when we are in danger of being too ego-centered and negatively self-centered? I have never lost the words of this dream, this particular statement by the Voice.

VII

The Dark and the Light
(1959–1962)

Almost three years after Mark Pelgrin's death, I faced surgery which might have revealed cancer. It didn't. I wrote this in the hospital:

> For five days I have been mostly body, with the spirit sitting quietly by, waiting. A body which is weak, malfunctioning temporarily, hurting—and a spirit which has only occasionally kindled. Tonight, after all visitors had gone, spirit felt so heavy, sad, weary. I need to say that this brush with death—for so it was as I experience it—heightens my sense of carrying something for Mark. And the lines of Psalm 118 come to me: "Though the Lord has indeed chastised me, yet he has not delivered me to death."
>
> This time I must wrestle with the angel until I am blessed—whatever that may mean. All nonessentials must be pared away. My illness and operation are like Balaam's ass. They show me the angel of the Lord when I can't see it.

On Christmas Eve I wrote:

> I am obsessed with Mark's operation and mine. What in the

unconscious is trying for expression? The irrational? The condition where the ego is not functioning? Where only the soul floats
in limbo? Where the mind does not, cannot, control the world?
Do I fear the letting go, the giving over?

The answer to these questions was slowly revealed over the
next few years.

The two days before the turning of year 1959 I had it out with
myself in my journal.

Is it true that it is not the pressure of outer things but our
attitude toward them that is wrong? Do I blame the outer demands when really I should be able to handle them if I could
come at them with love and joy? I seem to be torn between self-
renunciation and self-need. Which is the true path at this point?
Can I—or should I—put aside more resolutely my own demands
as egocentric and limited?

Is this feeling about needing time a false path, childish, foolish?
Who am I to ask time to go into the wordless world within?
I, like every other adult in the world, must take reality right
where it is! And it is in the life I have chosen, in my work, in
seminars, in writing, in trying to be a good friend, etc. So why
don't I accept it, realizing that I cannot forever go on saying
that it should be this way or that way! . . . Then when I look back
at my Zurich notes of work with Mrs. Jung I find references to
"letting go," to "moon consciousness," to timelessness. This
adds to the conflict. All this is fine in Zurich, but what about
here and now? My unconscious has quit giving me any help.
No dreams, no poems, no paintings—and no indication even
that they are in the making.

This having it out helped clear the air, and I could go forward
with life.

In 1960 I was again in Europe, mostly in Switzerland and
England. In London an intensive time of analysis with Dr. Ger-
hard Adler opened out to new realms. Many of the dreams and
other inner manifestations Dr. Adler and I worked with preceded
this time with him. Thus what follows comes from the time between December 1959 and June 1960—a good half-year of intensive dreaming (well over 200 dreams) and active imagination

work.

We began where I had left off in my journal many months before—with the problem of Time. Having had no real "mother" functioning in the first half of my life, the problem of time showed me two faces: (a) negative-mother time, transiency, transitoriness, melancholy, all this reinforced by my own buried (thus negative) intuition which darkly saw only doomsday with the passing of time, and (b) sun consciousness—a more masculine dimension—which because it could work well pulled me into intense work, never *wasting* time. Thus outer activity = being time-driven = escape from the anxiety of the negative mother (or) a masculine world adaptation.

Dr. Adler suggested that I try not to load outer activity with too many negatives, but that at the same time I try to see the archetypal conflict in me as the cause of the fear, rather than the work itself. And I must not move faster into the outer than the inner growth wished.

"The time has come for a new feminine willingness to life," he told me, "to Sophia as the highest wisdom. In the Hebrew Old Testament it says, 'We do, and we hear.' You need to move in a new direction, act, and then the understanding of it comes."

Among the first dreams we worked with were these:

(103)
In mountainous country are many women, among them myself and several friends. We are toiling up a slope when a huge hand, a feminine and cosmic hand, like a Quan Yin hand, white, beautifully graceful, reaches down from above and seems to lift the skin gently from each woman who is bent over and struggling upward. Each one, alone, has to meet her fate unclothed in her outer skin.

(104)
I am somewhere with a group of people when a terrible and cosmic storm breaks, with crashing bolts of lightning in the night sky. One or two others and I seek some shelter, although with real question as to whether we may not perish. We enter a small building for protection. Someone says, or I know, that the lightning bolts are really a white-hot fiery hand, as of God,

upon which we must not look directly. Then I am aware of a
necklace I am wearing, very long and strange and mysterious.
I feel it. It is alive, and its joined part is two entwined and
moving snakes. I also realize that the heads are fanged, poison-
ous, and dangerous if I make the wrong move. They will keep
me continuously aware of what I must do to serve some power
greater than I. They bare their fangs and retract them several
times until I learn that I am to set them free in some vines
above my head. I do. They climb into these and disappear. We
must wait quietly for what comes next. I now have around my
neck another necklace, like a third snake form, but symbolic.
Somehow I have some strange and frightening power working
through me.

[Later that same night] There is a black centipede-like creature
with green moss on it, about three inches long. It is related to
a "condition of complete simplicity."

Both (103) and (104) seemed to be related to being just who one
is, where one is—a counterpoise to my cruelty to myself via
drivenness. The great Hand of the Goddess serves to reveal us as
we are under our outer covering. The two-snake necklace and
then the single snake indicated a movement from the world of
healing, of Asklepios and the caduceus of two serpents, to the
world of Dionysus, of feminine mysteries, darkness, not-knowing.

Despite the archetypal nature of these dreams, they contain
concrete, everyday insights within their cosmic symbols: to let
go, to let life unfold, to stop pushing, to trust what comes from
within, to put my hands into the Hands of the Other, to wait for
strange beings such as serpents and for great Hands from unseen
places to guide me. The lightning bolts as masculine and the
snakes as feminine indicated my beginning awareness of the
archetypal mother and father supporting me. Perhaps I could
begin to let go of them as outer persons.

One of my most important dreams was this:

(105)
Somehow I know that people can choose when to die, except
that they also seem not to choose but to be chosen. I see different
people getting into the death machines—like metal capsules

which are closed over them—and then comes a brief flash and a puff of smoke and they are dead. Then I know I am to die the next day. I am afraid and terribly upset because suddenly there is no time left in my life. I think how horrible it will be in that moment when I am inside waiting for the death shock. I wonder why they do not give sedation. I wonder how to spend these last 24 hours. There is no one I know to be with. For awhile I sit at a table with six or seven other women. One complains about the food, and I say it is good. Over all else hangs this sense of impending death. Someone gives me a large honey tablet to keep me from coughing during the night so that I can sleep. This seems absurd because I am to die anyway. I have a sense of doom, of helplessness, of fear at this sudden end.

This dream put to me, very clearly, the fact that no mother figure, now or in the future, was going to save me. I had to choose to carry myself—or to be carried—through death to rebirth. This deeply disturbing dream marked the inevitable and terrible separation of my spirit from the body of the mother-daughter complex, so that the substance of my humanity and mortality could be cleansed and purified for a new birth.

It meant literally that I had to be conscious, at all times and in whatever relationships, of where I was tempted to seek escape from this imperative of "die to become." Where did I look for sedation? Where did I hope that someone or something would choose for me? Despite my years, my maturity in many areas, my competence in many areas, this *must* was a torment. It forced me to let go of many things I had clung to for safety, and I did not often let go so gracefully or graciously. I resented what life did to me. I fought against it. I felt put upon. But when I could let go and be a different person, the rewards were there.

It was good that at this time I had friends with me in London and that two of them were also working with Dr. Adler. We were forced to confront one another, to clarify our friendships, to understand and change our neurotic behavior.

One afternoon as I walked along the Thames, I kept saying over and over to myself, "I have to die. I have to die."

Then it came to me: But of course I do. The defensive desire to always be objective and undisturbed and above the human mess of feelings has to die.

I realized then that the greatest torture for me was being confused, emotional, upset, not knowing. I realized too that I had to sustain the tension of this archaic feeling until I was more related to it, and that part of my problem was not wanting to do this. Relationship of any kind has to be pain and suffering and desolation and endurance before it can be a pure gift. It was as if I had always equated pain with punishment, and therefore as evil and to be avoided.

Many of the past year's dreams began to come into focus for me: an ugly animal hide to be cured and softened; an emphasis over and over on the huge task, the great cost, the unbelievable slowness of the work; the going alone and naked; Jung's words, copied into my journal: "Wholeness is in fact a charisma which can be manufactured neither by art nor by cunning; one can only grow into and endure whatever its advent may bring"; the recurring idea of the unique, human, unorthodox ways that must be taken; the emphasis on losing the persona, getting down into the roots, the mud, the torn-up roads, the wetness, the absurdity; recurring dreams of not going by rules or "oughts" but by personal ways; and Neumann's words, "A strengthening of life can only be bought at the cost of a sacrificial death . . . The suffering entailed by the very fact of being an *ego* and an individual is implicit in the hero's situation."

All of these inner events and insights were, of course, going on in the midst of an outer life which held travels in England with my friends—seeing the lovely English countryside, its great cathedrals and universities, meeting and having a long tea-time with C. S. Lewis and his wife in Oxford, staying at such places as The Ancient Manor of God Begot, taking in the art galleries, theaters, concerts. Later we went on to Switzerland, Israel, and returned to London. Whatever was moving inside me had of necessity to be lived in the outer world. When I am intent upon the inner world as it moves into the outer one, the one thing I can be most sure of is that it will not be comfortable—but it *will* be exciting.

I was helped much by the loving, supporting letters from Harry
_____, my man in the United States. Should I marry him or
not? Dr. Adler and I talked of this several times, and he felt, as
I did most of the time, that marriage at this late date didn't seem
right for either of us. We had all the depths of relationship, but
each of us had forged out a way of life very differently. The
attempt to set up a single household could be difficult. (We never
married, but our relationship of love continued until his death
four years later.)

My dreams began to make statements about both the masculine
and feminine dimensions. Such dream figures as Maria, St. John,
God, Quan Yin, Queen, Monk, my dead mother, my father, and
the Pope of Darkness came along. Scattered in with these were
several dreams of the golden child, the fairy child, the fantasy
child. At the end of this series came dreams of: the snake between
the fanged one and the plain one is missing in evolution; I see
an arrow-pendulum sketch related to meeting life in the imme-
diate moment; a pelican who will destroy her nest in the center
unless one goes correctly from one side of the center to the
other.

As Dr. Adler and I pushed this series of dreams around, a message of centering emerged. He pointed out that with the snake
one is really submitting to the life-death forces and can only
wait unmoving. One is oneself the egg. But with the pelican,
the destruction will come only if the individual (me) threatens
the nest by going a wrong direction, i.e., by going through the
Center. Ego consciousness and ego choice is possible and is being
asked for. But the center is also me as Self. And this must be gone
into.

"Sometimes," Adler said with amusement, "the only answer is
just to go into the messy middle of things and sit there. There is
always insecurity in life, and to know this and accept this is absolutely necessary for wholeness."

He suggested that it might help if I actually made a circle and
sat in the middle of it for meditation. (I did, and it did.) He also
quoted what Jung had once said to him: "My psychology is an
either-and-or-psychology, I guess." It was precisely the either-

and-or that was struggling in me.

My dreams, exactly like my life, like anyone's life, go in waves as if the messages cannot get through without repetition because my inner unwillingness to grow is so strong. Suddenly I began being presented with images of the City. I had been much impressed by the writings of Charles Williams and his concern with the City. He wrote an article called *The Image of the City in English Verse*. Williams was one of the most prolific writers of his time and his novels and theological writings as well as his poetry had a great influence on T. S. Eliot, W. H. Auden and C. S. Lewis. For Williams the City is the symbol (although I do not believe he used that word) of kinds of order. I dreamt of the City in various moods:

(106)
I am with friends on a tour of exploration in a vast underground City. We see some elaborate beautiful ivory and silver carvings.

(107)
I am going around to the gates of (the same?) City, seeing various treasures and relating them to myself and my journey, somehow saying to myself that I want the permanent lasting things, not the cheap and perishable ones.

(108)
(As if this were the same City of the two preceding nights) In order to enter the City you have to knock with a wooden staff on the gate that belongs to the Goddess. Then you can enter and be shown what lies within, both of joy and of terror. The gate-keepers are male figures related to the Silenus of the Villa of Mysteries in Pompeii. There is also an image of the golden Babylonian goat on its hind feet. It seems as if, wherever I go in the underground streets and corridors, there are reminders pointing to the gates and the things involved in entering. There is some relationship between these gates, or this place where I am in the City, and Theobald's Road in London. There is a scene where I am with a male patient from America, trying to help him in some action or attitude toward the City—like being oneself, risking, etc.

Dreams (106) and (107) told of entrances and treasures. Ivory
and silver are like moonlight, feminine, delicate and subtle. But
also ivory comes from archaic animals and their phallic tusks—
so both masculine and feminine combine here. Dr. Adler and I
felt the gates were like the Ghiberti doors of the Baptistery in
Florence, Italy. These dreams told me that "outsideness" (the
terror), the moving-into-the-mess of feelings, was the vital "in-
sideness" for me now. What I had fled from I had to face. Only
this could knock down my defenses.

Dr. Adler asked, "Why do you resist your feelings that come
out so freely when you let them by way of music, poetry, sex,
nature?"

He told the story of a patient, a man who had many of the same
defenses, who had dreamed that he was a policeman and that
he arrested himself for wearing daffodils in his hat!

"You are like that," Dr. Adler told me bluntly. But his eyes
laughed, and so I laughed.

Dreams (108) above and (109) given below were turning points.
Goddess and wooden staff took me back to a very early dream
of a shut gate, a priestess and a cedar staff. Now entrance is possible, although it wasn't then. Also I can now lift the veil of the
temple, so to speak, and see the golden goat of Silenus. Christian,
Judaic, pagan—all came together. Part of my new destiny, I began
to understand, was to bring these three parts together somehow
within myself and my life. I knew it meant walking the razor's
edge between the discipline of consciousness and the free flow
of the instincts; between the Logos and Dionysus (Silenus), both
of which ask for discipline, surrender, active passivity, if identity
is to be established.

Identity, of course, is not an easy thing to come by. What is
our identity? Is it what we do? Say? Feel? Or is it something much
deeper and fuller than any of these? We cannot know it rationally,
I am certain, although many psychologies work for just this.
Materialistic existentialists like Sartre would say we create our
identity by our acts. Religious existentialists like Kierkegaard
would say that as we act, as we are in process of "being able,"
we are identified as part of God. We are always trying, and must

try, to identify ourselves—and we can never quite do it verbally or rationally. As I struggle for wholeness, genuinely and honestly, even if I resist I am constantly becoming part of that Other which is larger than I.

(109)
I am going to see the Cassetta Stone (or a stone of Cassetta marble) as it contained a clue to some mystery I need to solve. Connected with this, I was looking down into a newly excavated, square sarcophagus containing a statue of a woman in a fetal position. The statue was cradled in a delicate powder blue material. I felt it was Greek.

This dream described what was going on in analysis: the revelation, the birth or rebirth, of a new feminine dimension of consciousness, embryonic and virginal, yet to be lifted from its sarcophagus and discovered. But it lay behind the gates of the City. My mystery, at this point, was to be found in the Villa of Mysteries. I did paintings of the ivory and silver door, the staff of wood, the statue in the sarcophagus. I went over again the magnificent frescoes (in a book on the Villa of Mysteries) and I realized that the woman initiate, naked before the angel with the whip, nurtured by the priestess, is surrendering but is not abandoned. Her feelings are all held out freely for rebirth. She has no defenses left.

This particular trip and inner journey added another dimension which was one of the most important of my life. To write had been a dream of mine since adolescence. Then I had written poetry—not very good. A few adult poems had been published in college magazines. After Mark Pelgrin's death in 1956, a friend joined me in editing his lucid and honest account of the time of his dying, which was published by Routledge & Kegan Paul (London) a year after my work with Dr. Adler. Then, after the death of Linda Fierz in Zurich, I began working on what was later published as *A Magic Dwells*. I was working on this some of the time on this particular trip. I talked about these things with Adler. Also, about this time I had tea with C. S. Lewis and was pulled even more into the world of fantasy writing. These thinkers and philosophers were of great interest to me. Martin Buber had based his philosophy on the contention that man could achieve an intimate relationship with God through an intimate interrelationship with his fellow man and that each man's relationship with God and fellow man was distinct. He felt religion was experience, not dogma, and stressed personal responsibility.

A story that was told to illustrate this point concerned an aged pious man, Rabbi Susya, who became fearful as death drew near. His friend chided him, "What, are you afraid that you'll be reproached that you weren't Moses?" "No," the Rabbi replied, "that I was not Susya."

I told Adler of a fragment of dream having to do with hungry children, and another about an infant who would always be with me. Somehow, as Dr. Adler and I put all this together during the last hour I would have with him for several months (because of my travels), we sensed that I needed to write seriously. Perhaps the hungry children were crying out within me for some expression of their existence. Both hungry children and healing must be served, he cautioned: "They are not separate. They must be seen as one central emergency."

When my friends and I came to Israel, it was divided, Jerusalem split in two, with Jordan holding part of it, Israel the other part. We went first to Jordan and visited those places under Jordanian jurisdiction, then crossed between barbed wire fences on foot into the Israel part of Jerusalem. We saw cities and villages of the Old and New Testaments, walked along the shore of the Lake of Genesaret (Sea of Galilee) and in the markets of Nazareth—all scenes that stirred my imagination, giving me the final experiences I needed to write my favorite of all my books, *Joseph's Son*.

During our stay in Israel we met and talked with Erich Neumann (who died the following year), and one of my friends talked with Martin Buber, the renowned Jewish philosopher and educator.

When we reached Switzerland, I decided to stay outside of Zurich in Kusnacht—the small town where the Jungs lived, as well as other Jungians. The first dream I had in this small hotel overlooking the lake was that I was with Mrs. Jung and she said to me, "Begin writing, and do a little bit every day." So I wrote some every day, sitting by the lake in the sun, watching children play in the daisy-filled grass. I was writing my own active imagination, letting it flow from me wherever it wanted to go. Before I was finished with it, long months after I had reached home and returned to work, it was more than 400 handwritten pages.

I had not intended to write for anyone but myself, but one day a very eager and bookish friend of mine asked to read it and later told me that I had a children's novel. I cut it some, had it typed, sent it to Atheneum Publishers, and of all surprising things, it was accepted, with the to-be-expected changes. It was called *Knee-Deep In Thunder*. A few years later I wrote a second book, which was also published.

I tell this to give an example of how, out of the most difficult and desperate inner work, something emerged that was to be become an important avocation-vocation. Writing is really the daffodils in the hat for me, the delight, the joy of words, the expression of my deep feelings as nothing else is. I love to paint and to carve, but only for myself. In writing I can share my reticent emotional side seriously and fully. So the sacrifices, the tumults, the pain, the darknesses of the soul and spirit—they are all worthwhile when they lead into the deeper place of the Other.

VIII

Picking Up Stitches
(1963–1966)

In 1962 my two friends and I returned to Zurich; again in 1964–
1965 we went to Zurich for further advanced study, and took
ourselves to Egypt also. In 1964 I was saddened by the assassina-
tion of President Kennedy and fourteen deaths among families
and close friends, among them my Harry. Egypt deepened my
understanding and acceptance of this death as well as the others.
With so much loss there comes a sense of scatteredness and of
not being sure where you are or what you are doing. As always,
my dreams brought help and healing.

Shortly before we left Zurich for Egypt, I had seven dreams
about the Jungs, which anchored me in their rootedness and
concern for the values of the Self, and strengthened my courage
for the long journey to selfhood. One other important dream
was this:

(110)
*I am going some place where the most important person is to
be Madame Farnetta, the internationally known medium.*

Such a short dream to be so important—but it was. I had always

rejected mediumistic phenomena—as I had previously rejected
such things as graphology and astrology. Even before I quite
awakened from the dream I knew that the name meant Far Flung
Net. And what was a net? Protection, shelter, cover; also snare,
captivity, negative mother, labyrinth; goddesses of fate, the
weavers and spinners. Then I found the following words in Neumann's *The Great Mother:*

> The Goddess Net, the Lady of the West . . . "I am all that has
> been, and is, and shall be, and my robe no mortal has yet uncov-
> ered"; . . . goddess of magic and weaving, unborn goddess,
> originating in herself, she was worshipped with mysteries and
> lantern processions . . . primeval watery mass . . . like Hecate,
> she is opener of the way, holding the key of the fertility god-
> desses, the key to the gates of the womb and the underworld,
> the gates of death and rebirth . . . the personification of the
> eternal female principle of life which was self-sustaining and
> self-existent and was secret and unknown and all pervading.

The medium, whether or not I liked it, stood between the worlds
of the conscious and unconscious, bringing the unconscious into
consciousness in occult or eccentric ways. When I began to relate
all this to my horoscope, it said clearly that I had to listen more
carefully to those irrational planets Uranos, Neptune, Mercury,
Pluto, who are so badly aspected for me that they can only begin
to be creative through deep inner solitary work.

We left Zurich for Egypt in a snowstorm, touched down in
Athens in a light and gentle rain, and arrived in Cairo under a
full moon on a warm evening. It was an auspicious start for an
amazing time: the ancient monumentalness of Egypt, the great
columns of temples raised up into the blue sky, their loveliness
and their overpowering magnitude, the Nile, the roadside scenes
so like Biblical ones that we felt moved millenia back in time,
our wonderful archeologist guide who watched over us like a
mother, the long train journey from Cairo to Luxor during which
we saw Egyptian villages and activities as they were centuries
ago.

Ancient Egypt passionately honored the dead—with pyramids,
with deep, richly carved shafts leading to tombs far below the

earth's surface, with temples and statues, with gold and turquoise treasures. Also, Egypt, contemporary, was callous toward death, of person or beast, because death, even smashing accidental death, was the will of Allah. And women were still the lowest of all beings, almost. These extremes jarred me into new awareness.

The visit to Egypt also helped me see my dark sister, my shadow side, in its creative aspects. Here is what I wrote in my journal early in 1965:

Journal

The matter of my dark side began with a dream about a badly sunburned baby needing oil = *the danger of not enough shade or darkness.* Then the dream of the terrible force of the point of light in the darkness, pulling me and my shadow toward it = *the need to enter into the darkness with Love in order to redeem something.* The clashes between blacks and whites = *the unreconciled shadow.* A black woman librarian being honored = *seeing the dark feminine as the keeper of wisdom.* A young black woman guitar teacher = *a dark vital gypsy side who can teach me.* A dream of being in Egypt and of coming out of Egypt = *the need to go into and return from the Mother.* A dream of making a huge animal-human drawing and filling it in with black = *the need to see all the darkness of primitive gods as part of my life.* Finally, the dream of following a dark-haired, red-robed cousin into a deep underground place = *the need to go with a risking, unconventional, shadow side of my family.* Then there have been dreams of ascents and descents, of my mother, father, brother, of my own health, of returning home.

As I struggle with all these, with the shadow, I begin to see that this land of Egypt really constellates my problem of my own shadow as opposed to, different from, the *machine animus* (also mine). It is sharply stated here in the terrible opposites of the gentle delight of the people, especially the younger ones, and the animals, and on the other hand, the terrible indifference toward life, the killing and injuring of animals by autos carelessly driven, the dying of people untended, etc.

My *creative shadow* is free and carefree, with irrational feelings, gypsy living, a subjective forward movement, excitement, intuitive leaps, without fear, mediumistic, not always counting the cost, warm, willing to laugh. My *machine animus* is cold,

driving, wants precision and order and rightness, wants life to
be rational, is critical and derogatory of all that is contrary to
order and precision.

Now my Shadow must be allowed to live centrally with me,
regardless of the risks this involves and the loss of long-held
ego images.

During our travels in Egypt, keeping up with the outer life
and the inner life as well was almost impossible. The days were
long, fascinating, and tiring. Even so, my inner world managed
to surface from time to time:

(111)
*I am being examined by two doctors, one woman and one
man, both of them tall, fair, Swiss. Then I am led down a ramp
and am with a very dark male doctor, Nubian or Egyptian.
He is small, gentle, I trust him. He takes me into a room to wait,
then he comes back and asks if I can return tomorrow because
he must go at once on an emergency to operate on a black man
who has come down in a space capsule and is blind. I say I
will return after the holidays. He says just to rest when I need to.*

Here it is the dark-skinned healer—the "shadow" healer—who
seems the gentler, and also the more mysterious because he is the
one who must deal with my blind and wounded shadow animus
from the unconscious depths (outer space). During this same
period I had a hypnogogic image, just before sleep, of a male
figure resembling the Egyptian god Ptah, with a skullcap on and
holding a staff, and I knew that his name was St. Ancient.

(112)
*I am participating in some ritual related to Egypt. One has to
begin by being carried by a goddess (or her image) into some
place, and then you come out from this place carrying a smaller
image—perhaps her child.*

I had to see that I must give myself over to be carried by the
Great Dark Goddess. Only if I could learn to do that would I
then be able to become a carrier of her Child, the smaller, more
personal feminine being which is a part of my darker side.

(113)

*I found and was showing to friends several beautiful Egyptian
scarabs which I had almost forgotten that I had. One was surrounded by a filigree of silver, one was in rose quartz, one had
gold on it. One was slightly marred because I hadn't handled
it carefully because I hadn't remembered I was carrying it.*

This was a strong warning. The Egyptian scarab beetle, sacred
because it lays its eggs under the earth and the new beetles emerge
from the earth as if reborn, is everywhere carved on temples,
pillars, walls. A very large Scarabeus is on a pedestal beside the
sacred lake at Luxor. In my dream all the rich alchemical colors
of transformation are there, all of the colors of rebirth—and yet
I have damaged part of my treasure because I did not remember
I had it. To forget what you have as inner treasure is one of the
worst sins against the unconscious. This dream was followed by
one in which very negative men had abducted and imprisoned
me, with no escape possible. The negative masculine oppressor
was moving in—ruling out the irrational, the playful, the spontaneous.

The stay in Egypt stirred things up, both on the positive and
negative sides. But the depths were moved, pushed into new
places, old things knocked loose. Shortly after I returned to the
United States and the working world I dreamed:

(114)

*I am with my brother. We go into a place where, amid corridors
and scenes of confusion, I see Harry coming toward me. He
opens his arms and I walk into them joyfully. My brother disappears. Harry and I are then in our bedroom, and soon are
intensely involved in beautiful and exciting lovemaking. He
is tender and passionate and creative, as is our love.*

Despite the poignancy of this dream, it was a deep affirmation
of what was going on in me. It helped me to feel less unsettled,
to feel I had not lost what we had had together.

I experienced a difficult reentry to the United States, seminars,
patients, and all of the usual (and unusual) problems of day-to-
day living. The seminars during weekends and then throughout
the summer had to be led; we were training new leaders and

had to work with them; and I was trying to be faithful to my writing. At the end of this too-busy summer I had this dream:

(115)
It's as if I were watching a medieval play, in costume, about a king. But also I am the king. A young man threatens me with his sword and I kill him with a dagger. Later on I kill a second one. Then I am with friends, when I see four young men, friends of those I killed, sneaking around to throw daggers at me and kill me. I am terrified, and wake myself up in my attempts to escape.

What a warning such dreams are! They pay little or no attention to all the fine things we've done (as I had been performing very successfully). They proceed to tell us what is wrong. And here the balance was all off. My inner King had gotten out of hand—from the point of view of my Self—and I was being chided. Having learned not to ignore these dream statements, I managed to get some time for myself, both at a beach place I shared with friends, and at Yosemite, always a restorative place of high mountains, still lakes and tall trees.

Within the next month several dream statements counteracted the negativity of the King:

(116)
I am with a young girl, of whom someone said, "She is clear and still as a mountain pool." Also I meet and talk with a nun—not in her habit. And the waking thought was that I, too, need to be a sort of nun looking after the children of various kinds.

This is self-explanatory. However, I began having and continued to have through the years many dreams of nuns and of being a nun. I believe such dreams tell me that essentially I am a solitary—not in a neurotic but in a creative sense. Surely my horoscope, with so many planets in the eighth and twelfth houses, tells me that I must do much inner work quietly and alone. My writing does this for me. For many years now I have had my own cabin at the Guild seminar center in the mountains, where I spend more and more time surrounded by my painting, writing and carving materials, and my dog. Here I am at peace.

To return to the dreams that followed the King (115):

(117)
*I am going down into a long tunnel of some sort, deep down
into the earth, to get to some professor in order to finish an
assignment. I am having to descend against an uprising flood
of rushing water.*

Again the theme of water, but here it is rising strongly from the
depths. Obviously, if I am to know what my work is to be, I
must go down, an absolute countermotion to being a killing King.

(118)
*I have to play a piece of music on a piano for an audience.
I have not practiced, don't really know the work, and do a poor
job. One of my friends, herself a fine pianist, is in the audience.*

This dream, I suspect, said: Quit trying to perform, and you are
not ready for it.

The last dream came exactly one month from the "King"
dream:

(119)
*I am riding a bicycle in Italy, just over the border from Switzer-
land. There are scenes of a hearty peasant man giving me a
gift of a bottle of wine—sort of a bon voyage present—with a
card whose message is in earthy Swiss humor; of being in a shop
in a station trying to buy a newspaper in Italian money, and
having only a handful of small Swiss coins which a smiling
Italian woman sorts over to find the right amount; and of a
very nice old lady who needs to return to Zurich and I help her
to find the right train.*
*Then I see a large beautiful map of Italy, its boot surrounded
by the waters of many seas, and in the middle of Italy there is
a huge mountain from which one can see in all directions for
hundreds of miles. I am bicycling up this great mountain in
order to get to the top. I go into a shop. While there I see an
elevator at the back of the shop. I ask a young man if it goes to
the top. He is new, he says, and doesn't know. But a woman
who works there says it does—but advises against my returning
from the mountain on the outside, on the road, for it is very
dangerous because of its height, the extreme cold, the icy over-*

hangs. But, she says, the view from the top is unsurpassable. She tells the young man how to take me up inside the mountain.

I follow him outside, then to an enormous castle, hundreds of stories high, with thousands of windows. There are great stairs leading up to the entrance. (It is as if the castle and the mountain are one, and going up to the castle would lead to the top of the mountain.) We enter. Some woman says all the windows must be washed, because it is out of season. Only servants are there now. The castle is very luxurious, and I see skis, tennis rackets, etc., for the rich who come during the high season. The rest of the dream is spent climbing, sometimes inside the castle, sometimes outside on funiculars with tremendous views of snow-capped peaks.

Certainly I had made a long journey from the negative King dominating me to this incredibly vast and beautiful overlook at the heights of the Vision of the Self. Such blessed views open up from time to time, when I need them and when I begin to see that I need them. They do not show me where I am but where I could begin to be if I lent my life to the journey. I am so reluctant to do this even when I have learned in past situations that such lending takes me always to a greater height, to a broader outlook. It delights me that this theme of earthy peasant people seems to go along with vistas of seeing. It takes the bicycle, the wine, the Swiss humor (never too subtle), the warm Italian temperament, and, from the Ego, both the desire and the willingness to make the Journey—really to travel, not just to know about, the Journey.

During 1966–1967 I finished my first juvenile novel, *Knee-Deep in Thunder* and worked hard on other writing as well. I began to have symptoms in bones and joints, later diagnosed as rheumatoid arthritis, which contributed to certain aspects of my maturing, of accepting myself with limitations. I went for the first time to the Grand Tetons; this trip underlined my deep love for mountains, my relationship to nature since childhood, and how I needed to honor this, live with it and in it, let it express itself in my writing.

Several important dreams came to me at the end of a busy summer of seminars, after we had decided once again to travel to our beloved Zurich, and to include a leisurely time in the Greek

Islands.

(120)
*I had to make a great mandala, octagonal in shape. Light
flowed from it in sweeping rays. I knew it had to do with clues
to understanding the mysteries of the Book of the Zohar.*

I knew little or nothing about the Zohar until I had this dream,
although I must have read something about it at some time during
my studies in Zurich. The dream came to me the night after I had
been writing a great magic scene in one of my stories and had
been reading Arthur Waite's book on magic, *The Book of Ceremonial Magic.* The Zohar, a Jewish-Spanish kabbalist book from
the Middle Ages, described the hidden world of the Godhead by
way of allegory and symbol. It also described a feminine element
in the Godhead, the Shekinah as ambivalent light and darkness,
and stressed that the purpose of rituals was to bring unity between the above and the below. This idea of the Godhead as
feminine as well as masculine was new and exciting to me. In
this intensely numinous dream, the strange light coming from
the octagonal mandala flowed mysteriously as if its energy would
never end.

(121a)
The words, "Change travels nowhere."

(121b)
The words, "Now and when I was loved by my heart."

These two dreams emphasized the Nowness of being, an
emphasis I needed because I could so easily be pushed by what
there was to do the *next* moment. Thus I needed to be told that
continual change does not lead anywhere, and that *now* is really
when the heart can love the Self.

(122)
*I am climbing in wild country with a group. We have to en-
counter a terrible man who practices evil sorcery. There are
two mountains ahead of us—one black and burned over, one
bright green from rains. At the foot of the black one there are
sad and tormented people crying out for water. I see the sorcerer*

*casting a spell over a man. Sparks leap from the sorcerer's
eyes and the man falls, screaming. Others are struck down.
Somehow I know that only love, held to with enormous strength
of will, can overcome this evil. In the end we are able to withstand the sorcerer, and we have some ritual procession.*

This dream contrasted the opposites always working in me—
the evil animus vs. love. Although these opposites are still there—
and probably always will be—I believe that I now have a greater
stockpile of love with which to fight the evil sorcerer. Related
to this thought is an excerpt from my journal written while in
the Grand Tetons.

Journal

Walked in this grandeur and pondered what it would be like to
be purged of egocentricities. As I pondered I felt freer. I began
to get a dim sense of what it could be to be unfettered, to be
unwanting, except only to serve the will larger than mine. The
lines of Edward Carpenter came to me: of dying being the reason
for living. And I thought of what I need to let go of in order to
be reborn. All those things I cling to, either as escapes or as reasons for existing, things I would not have if I were in a solitary
prison cell: the written and the printed word; the sight and sound
of those I love; birds and animals; photography; music; all collec-
tions of rocks, feathers, etc.; any plans for anything; reputation
and achievement. I'm sure there are others.
    Then I thought what I'd have left in that prison: God's pres-
ence; physical life; the ability to love; memories. And if I could
pare my existence to those things alone I would be rich. So then,
if I can let go of these parts of my life that hinder me, how light
and how free! I could move toward my essential purpose as God
intends it. I want to do this!

And on the last day of the year, shortly before we left again
for Europe, I wrote:

Journal

Almost a year's end, under a cool blue windy sky. It's been a
strange and growing year—strange because of unexpected things
like a novel accepted and new physical limitations, growing in

self-acceptance, in lessened egocentricity and anxiety, in deepened maturing relationships.

I've pulled in a bit, written more, perhaps been more myself.
Time and transiency trouble me less, thus perhaps I can move
into these later years with more inner peace. More often I savor
moments of life with a quiet pleasure—although I still do not find
it easy to feel *joy*.

And this is my greatest longing for the new year of 1967: to
feel joy, the abundant joy. It can enliven me, illumine my love,
enrich my days.

One of the ways I can do that is to remember Charles Williams'
words, "All luck is good."

IX

Divinities and Devils
(1967–May 1969)

The year 1967 opened with a predictive dream:

(123)
I am in some way as if I were pregnant. I am in pain, moaning and bearing down, knowing I'm not really physically pregnant but wondering what is happening, what will come out. Others are around.

Then a scene where _____ (a young woman patient of mine) is trying to run some group by bringing into it all sorts of people who do not belong—too young, hostile, unready— and I am trying to get rid of them.

In retrospect, my "pregnancy" indicated that many new attitudes were in the making, but also my unconscious feminine side was pushing too hard and not being fully responsible, just as this young woman was doing in her life. In fact, she became pregnant and forced a marriage which, some years later, proved a real mistake.

I knew that the arthritis with its pain and limitation and enforced rest was trying to tell me something. My old ego had been again too much on the side of keeping on and keeping up, living up to, never letting anyone or anything down. At the same time, naturally, my dark other was becoming angry, hostile and frustrated. Dream (123) told me these things, that the "ought-to" and the "rebel" side were beginning to have at each other, that I had better watch out.

That year, shortly after our arrival in Zurich to give and attend seminars came these dreams:

(124)
I am going somewhere for some important event. Am I prepared? Or must I go just as I am?

(125)
Something about a new car—that it must have power steering and some sort of gay or colorful ornamentation.

I am with a group acting out the problem of evil—pantomiming in "slapstick" fashion, clowning around a pool, throwing things in it. I partly disapprove and partly like what is happening.

On a buslike vehicle with K_____, going on some very long trip. Bus is crowded. Conductor (woman) asks for fare. I pay for myself but can't find my companion. I finally find her, peacefully sleeping. I decide to let her rest, and get her money later. I find empty deck chairs in the sun and decide to rest there. It will be a long trip.

My unconscious was giving me several messages. Perhaps I was only partly ready, and that meant that I needed to go just as I was. I needed to go with consideration for my body, as well as my psyche. Also (125) told me I needed to have a power steering, an ease of guidance, without strain, and with some gaiety. The new way of going needed to be with joy—not exerting my power but letting a greater power work.

I was also being told that perhaps evil (mine and the world's) was to be dealt with both seriously and with laughter, that the Fool needed to be along. Finally, I needed to see that the Journey was long, that I had just enough libido to carry me from day to day, that rest was necessary. The feminine conductor (125) was relaxed enough to say pay after you've rested. I did not do too well in heeding these warnings.

Despite Europe and my love for it, especially for Switzerland, I could not fight off a subtle depression that had been with me since my illness—although not necessarily caused by it. One dream talked of the fact that black was the best color for the Journey. Then the very next night:

(126)
I'm in some village and a big, fat, coarse German has power over me—as if I were a slave to him, or a prisoner—and he is making me beat to fragments some small object of art. I fear him, feeling he will always be coming to make me do something like that. Then I am singing in the village square—while I am working—and I am wondering how I can outwit him so I won't have to destroy again.

Clearly this was my well-known driving and cruel Saturn that caused me depressions, doubts, emptinesses, destructiveness, and self-negations. Earthy work and singing could perhaps win out, but it wouldn't be easy.

One important trip at that time was to visit friends in Geneva for a weekend. It was cold, with rain and snow. One Saturday afternoon I walked alone along the lake, and then went again on Sunday morning. My experience there on that wintry day I have never forgotten. My journal describes best where I was and what I felt:

Journal

A rainwet city; cold birds flying; my body aches; there is a weight of sadness touched off by a dream of needing to go away some-where. Then the music of the bells resounding over the lake and throughout the world. And swans, idly courting one another and letting long necks sink into the water for food. Five ducks diving at once and then surfacing like five corks popping. Clouds and mists over sharp hills, and snow, and the cathedral like a litho-graph against a pearl background.

And through and in and out and within and over all this—me wandering and lonely, asking about myself and all my lacks, and from there asking about humans, these beasts with burnished heads teeming with dreams and cruelties, poetry and war, great-ness and horror.

I am depressed and empty, sensing life as a perpetual dying. Then I am moved into a sadness more creative because less lost and I have tears rather than holes where my eyes look at the view.

Not too long before we left for Greece, several events (including dreams) contained rich meaning. First, a dream:

(127)
I am inside a medieval walled city. There are enemies out-side, and I have to put myself between them and a wise old man to protect him with my body in some way. Also, there is some incident having to do with ancient and beautiful stone carvings in this city.

Clearly, the ego must be used to guard that which is larger than itself, in this case a wisdom figure similar to Mercurius Senex—that aspect of Mercury who in alchemy is related to transformation, the essential inner being, god of revelation, the archetype of the spirit. But the ego must make sacrifices to guarantee wholeness. Jung points out in *Psychology and Alchemy* that because Mercury tends to flee, he must be sealed within a temenos.

Mercury is also Saturn, or Satan, as the old man, the ambiguous god, the light of nature. For me, this Mercury Senex was also related to Jung himself because of the stone carvings in the dream. I had seen Jung's own carvings in stone at Bollingen. The old man was, for me, also related to the ancient knowledge held by some old shaman. Thus the dream was saying that the ego no longer serves itself but acts to keep the worldly enemies from attacking the inner knowing. It must care, in a feminine dimension way, about wholeness. For me, at that time, the dream meant that my ego must stop serving itself by any "oughts" and collective pulls, and must guard the inner city, its work of individuation, its healing gods.

One more very simple and important dream before Greece:

(128)
Someone gave me a book titled Ulysses, Volume 2.

Such a simple dream it was, with such a wealth of associations.

I had had adolescent fantasies of Ulysses and his men tied to the mast to help them resist the Sirens. After long analytic discussions of these fantasies with others and even longer ponderings about them myself, it comes to me now that they relate to my separation from the feminine dimension I described earlier, my fear of being seduced by it, as my mother perhaps feared it and sacrificed it.

The masculine dimension in me had to fight off unconsciousness (as Ulysses and his men had to do) lest it overcome me. My second association was with Fritz Kunkel's telling (in a seminar) of Ulysses and of how Penelope remained faithful to him throughout his wanderings. I had also recently read Kazantzakis' sequel to the Odyssey, in which he selected Ulysses the Wanderer as his hero image of the twentieth century. Of course, I also knew James Joyce's novel, *Ulysses*, a breakthrough in the modern novel form with its stream of consciousness. With all this going around in me, the dream, simple though it was, held multiple implications of the meaning of the Journey.

The night we reached Athens I received my orders from the inner dreamer:

(129)
I am separate from my body—or at least from my head and its face. I am looking at my face from outside it. The eyes are open, the mouth serious. I take my hands and push my lips out at the corners. I have an eerie sense of how "I" feel compared to the expression of the face—and prepare (decide?) to get back inside "me."

Was this saying to get back into the body, to let the spirit bring the body to joy? Is the flesh here forsaken? And the ego must return to its friend, the flesh? So it seemed. Greece was a good place to do these things, although the first dream after we arrived seemed to belie this:

(130)
I meet my dear friend _____. She is in deep mourning, black veils cover her face, because she has just learned that her favorite grandson has fallen from a tree and been killed. I try

to console her. Somewhere are the words—written or spoken—
"all flesh (or creatures) is born to be forgotten." We are in rain,
snow, darkness.

She is, like I am, fearful of her feelings. She wants friendship,
however, and her love for husband and children is real and warm.
She has no grandson. I felt that this dead child was that child in
me which had so early died, and that here the deepest mother-
feelings were being expressed for the lost and irreplaceable (in
its old form) child-spirit of joy.

The Greek Islands, nonetheless, did open the door to the child-
spirit of joy—as well as to inner dark spirits, storms, cruel men,
near disasters. Outwardly the seas were, on the whole, kind. It
was as if the outer history and beauty of these Islands, and all of
the myths related to them, stirred the outer imagination and also
the inner unconscious responses. My feelings were running high,
and for me that was wonderful indeed, as these extracts from my
journal show.

Journal

The insight about the buried child of joy in dream (130) is crucial.
There is truly a chance of being born again of water and the
spirit, I believe. And I am beginning, just barely, to see what it
would be like to live life so that, with Charles Williams, I know
that "all luck is good." "Holy luck" is what adds up to an existence under the Omnipotence. And holy luck and joy are god-
children to the wandering Son of man.

Yesterday's long boat trip—nine hours—was holy luck. It
meant a sense of Greece and Greeks, of the wine-dark and fierce
Aegean with its teeth showing, of seeing the little ports of Syra
and Tinos, of riding the launch into Myconos in a dark rolling
sea, of falling asleep to the sea roar outside my windows.

Today I am propped against a stone wall, sheltered from the
cold north wind. To my right, westerly, lies Delos—ancient
sleeping birthplace of Apollo.

A year ago, seeing the far beach, the terraced hills, the wind-
mills, the shining white village, I would have been restless to
explore. Now I cannot, and I know it, and after only a brief
moment of regret, I accept it. I even see that this can be holy
luck—if I follow it in and down to some deeper source. To be

XII.   The library at Four Springs, Middleton, 1972

XIII.   The Fool, painting by Sheila Moon, 1979

this physically tired and limited is often painful, sometimes irksome. Sometimes also it falls upon me suddenly that I don't have to do always. I can just be.

[Later] I must remember this scene and this quality of being! If all machines died and all time-measurers ended now, life would go on in glorious reality—burros and boats would be there, and a man flailing a squid to tenderness, arcing it over his head in a dancer's rhythm and bring it down—*squap*—like a comet on a seawet rock, and two Sunday men using hand lines from the jetty, and warm sun and west wind, and bells on beasts and churches.

It would not matter at all that machines were dead. Time would once more become what it was intended to be—a way of saying "The cock crows," or "It's time to rest and eat," or "Sun has set and let's go home," or "I love you," or "See how the grapes have grown."

This kind of time can be kept. I am beginning to see this. It will be possible but not easy. Only if I remember. And find it. (It must exist, even in America.) There is healing in this sort of time—and peace. It is like having bread and cheese and wine and sunlight. As simple as that.

When we returned to the States shortly after the Greek trip, I moved into a summer filled with seminars, many people needing help, much work to do. One novel was finished and published, and the sequel well under way. Yet all was not well with me. As I look back, I believe that neither my psyche nor my body was ready to go back to that world of seminars, therapy, writing. Perhaps because I had not worked analytically during this trip. Perhaps because something in me was ready to break out, and would have broken out even if I had been with an analyst. Perhaps it was time for a breakthrough—as does happen to us, whether we're ready or not.

I wasn't ready to face the extremes of the masculine dimension problems in me, but the next two years forced me to do so. I believe the first dream indication of what was coming was given me while I was still in Greece:

(131)
A friend and I are watching two men riding spirited horses.

*We see that the men are using cruel bits in the horses' mouths,
and also spurs, and even a short pole with a cruel hook at
the end. One man pulls on the bit and hooks the horse's leg. I
am horrified. The horse rolls on the man, and I think the horse
is hurt and has hurt the man. I hope it has. But the horse struggles up and the man again begins his cruelty. My friend and I
are horrified, and I prepare to do something about it.*

This dream got set aside in the wonder and excitement of Greece,
and I did not see its significance until several months later when
I began to get other similar messages. For example:

(132)
*I'm supposed to sing in a church service, but get hopelessly lost
and am rushing through water, snow, over cliffs, etc. And then
I am with a doctor friend, and he is checking my heart and
warning me that I am doing too much, and I realize I am very
very tired.*

(133)
*I am in a big house with others. There is a sense of eerieness
and fear. We are in a small room, hiding. I am very afraid of
some mystery beyond my comprehension having to do with
three spheres of existence—one above ours, one below ours,
and ours. The above and the below ones had unseen forces
acting upon us. Like in some of the Charles Williams worlds.
I must go out into these worlds, and I am resisting going. (They
are personified by unseen voices, one a deep rich bass, the other
an unearthly high soprano.)*

(134)
*Some man who has been a criminal is now part of a group
that includes me. I say he looks better—but I have misgivings
about him.*

(135)
*I drop Harry's watch, it breaks open and its jewels—dozens
of seed pearls—scatter about. Is it ruined? (I wakened recalling
the dream of the broken watch just preceding a previous operation.)*

(136)
Some scene of a terrible accident, with children run over, and

a man picking one up and shaking it cruelly, probably when it is terribly hurt or dead.

Then I feel paralyzed, prone, being drawn by some dark power into a dark room. I keep saying aloud, "O God, O Mother, Mother, O God," and I feel that this saved me.

Dreams (131), (134) and (136) all deal with a cruel and negative masculine dimension part of me, a part that is not manifested in cruelty to others but in a demonic cruelty to my own deepest being. I believe that (133) held a clue—my resistance to going into the mystery. As long as I resist plunging into the unknown levels of my existence I am at the mercy of the dark powers. Dream (136) gave a better resolution to the demonic power—the affirmation of that which stood over against it, God the Mother. My own mother had feared her dark side too much ever to help me with darkness. The greater Mother was needed. Dreams (132) and (135) warned what could happen to me and to my "time" if I did not stop and listen.

A journal entry toward the end of summer indicates that I was at least wondering, even if I did not yet seem to be inward enough.

Journal

This morning as I sat outdoors listening to Poulenc's "Gloria," finding that I was torn with sadness and other feelings too vague to recognize and that tears were there, I realized how often of late this has been true. So many things that once I would have taken boldly and with a false objectivity, during these last weeks have borne in on me with a weight of emotion I wouldn't have believed. Is it because I am not at the peak physically, because the aging process is making itself felt? Because I am not doing the creative things?

Somehow I feel that none of these questions, although they come to mind from time to time, is relevant.

In some strange way, I feel that I am in a very new responsiveness, a critical one, to my entire world, outside and inside, that some fresh sorting of values is going on, some reassessment of what is going on in me, in others, in the twentieth century.

I care more than I ever have about the evolution of humans, about where the "Son of man" is in individuals, about whether we will manage to blow ourselves up or if we can learn in time who we could be. I am concerned about the terrible extremes confronting us on every side—the Peace Corps and the genocide of Vietnam; the conquest of space, and the pollution of it; the advances of medicine, and death on the highways; the availability of books to everyone via paperbacks, and the incredibly low level of most of them and of all mass media.

And now I am aware that my deepest involvement is with those polar opposites of, on the one hand, the increase of concern for "togetherness" and "love" (especially by the younger generation, and especially by those members of it who are walking away from the Establishment and trying to find another set of values), and, on the other hand, the abuses and irresponsibilities of many of the methods used (sexual license, drugs, withdrawal from the world of reality). It seems to be absolutely essential if "planetization" (to use Teilhard's word) is to take place that we learn to live together in love, in mutual respect and dignity and kinship.

It also seems essential that this, if it is to be implemented, means the abandonment of many of the values of the dominant culture.

As a member of the older generation, I want to do everything I can to embrace the creative and original values of the young— including new attitudes toward sex and love. At the same time I refuse to be bullied into assuming that the exploitations of one person by another (the reduction of sex to a quick happening that's fun or to an appetite that is no different from hunger or fatigue) are creative relationships.

I refuse also to be bullied into assuming that anyone is old-fashioned who doesn't accept the so-called mind-expanding drugs as the modern way to self-knowledge. I grant that my own evil is deep and strong. I am well aware that drives and desires and compulsions exist in me as in most people. But if I assume that I should follow them only as I want to—in this sense to be uninhibited—I would also be assuming that other people did not matter. I would be renouncing the highest function of a human— the reflection on my actions and their consequences. I would be assuming that self-indulgence stands above self-knowledge.

And in all this wandering about in myself, and in current values I am trying to sort out, I keep wondering what, of the many things I am doing, are the most creative ones. And what ones are uncreative and should be junked.

Toward the year's end came two of the terrible dreams again, with a lovely counterirritant in between them.

(137)
I am in bed, and a man comes in, belonging to me somehow, awful. I seize him and try to overpower him, knowing that he is evil. *He vomits milk as he tries to overpower me. I get away from him and go outside the room, finding myself in a building filled with sick and dying people, everyone trying to reach a phone for help. Too many people and too few phones. I try to go outside the building. The streets are filled with people collapsing and dying from a choking fog that is everywhere. (I wakened in terror, thinking that I heard a voice in the hall. And I turned on my radio and heard an announcer saying, "This is your hour and the power of darkness.")*

This was one of the most dreadful dream experiences of my life. I was so shaken by it that I could not sleep the rest of the night. The final words are those said at Jesus' betrayal in Gethsemane. I struggled to see what they meant for me, hoped deeply that such a dream would not come again.

The in-between dream was a great comfort:

(138)
I recall a poem _____ Do hazelnuts in the woods glisten as they grow? Or do the nuts I seek _____?_____?
  Then I know I had seen a nest-like place, either with nuts in it or where nuts could be—and I know it is spiritual nuts that I am seeking.

I love hazel nuts. One of my favorite mystical passages is where Juliana of Norwich describes her experience of the Other as "no larger than an hazel nut," and that "it be all there is." I began to see then that the kernel of meaning for me must be sought for both in nature and in the *contra naturam* of the inward way, and its smallnesses.

The other terrible dream was this:

(139)
There is some evil young man that we are trying to contain.

Once I have my hands around his throat. I know that I can kill him—but I also know that this is not the way to deal with him.

It says exactly what it means. I must deal with the evil and the darkness. I cannot wipe it out.

On the eve of the new year, always a time of mysterious ends and beginnings, the dream given me had in it the ultimate meaning of healing of the wounds from the negative and destructive masculine:

(140)
Three women come to me. They come like the three magi—in a procession, wearing crowns, and carrying gifts. Yet with all this they were very feminine, very human and ordinary.

I felt this was about those who come from afar seeking the new birth in me. I related it to the three periods of my life and of my Journey, as a feminine dimension trinity of queenly aspects— perhaps, I thought, bringing perfume, fruit, and clothes for deaths and births.

This dream, with its true resolution, was not yet assimilated by me so that it could resolve. More dreams of the masculine evil or demonic figures came along all during 1968 and in early 1969. It was not until the spring of 1969, when again I was in Europe to recharge my inner energies, that I was able to work through them to newer and deeper understandings. I discuss them in the next chapter.

In 1968 I worked as therapist, college professor, and seminar leader, struggled with health, survived the death of my father, and finished my second novel. I began again, after a long dry time, to find writing poetry a real and definite expression of my difficult psyche.

The last dream I had before arriving in Zurich in May 1969 was the classic dream of all those concerning my evil masculine:

(141)
On a large table, on the top of a pile of reading material, is a very large and impressive book with the title The Plunder of Time, *and its author was Satan.*

With this I returned to the deep inner work.

X

Facing the Demon of My Life (May 1969–March 1970)

Journal

At this point, I seem to have an empty larder, the harvest is used up, it is a time of emptiness. The need is driving me to give up as many possessions as possible. Outer ones—books, clothes, paintings, for example—but much more important is to give up wanting the "right" things for others, or wanting others to behave in certain ways. And most important of all possessions to give up are the images others have of me (and thus images I must have encouraged)—such as being always able, tireless, disciplined, creative, witty, intellectual, brusque, unfeeling, sensate, concentrating on one thing or person at a time, extremist, autonomous.

If I really could be dispossessed of all these, what would I have left? Love of the Cry, of God, and the purposes of that Cry in any direction. I could let others be and do exactly what they choose to be and do. I could live simply and uncluttered. There would be time for prayer, for enjoying nature, for laughter. There would be no concern for achievement of any kind. I could let my work be service to the larger Purpose wherever it seems to need me most. I would never have to be anxious about tomorrow, would never need defenses because there would be nothing to defend.

My two friends and I went to Europe in March, coming to the
lovely and then still unspoiled coast of Portugal—the Algarve—
long beaches with fishing boats rolled into the sea on logs, pushed
by the sailors, a coast filled with grottoes and caves, crabs and
other sea creatures. From the cliffs above the sea near our hotel
we watched a school of great whales blow and surface, dive and
surface, in a wonderful arcing dance. And we saw a little group
of schoolchildren—none over eight years old—carrying from the
home to the church the body of a friend who had died, secured
in her child-sized casket. This, we were told, was an old Portu-
guese custom. How early one must learn death in this peasant
wisdom! We drove a small, wired-together, aged automobile
through the countryside, through groves of cork oak trees, to
castles, through small villages, for picnics. We sat in the sun,
and swam, tending our inwardness. It was good preparation for
our beginning work in Zurich.

The inner dreamer did its work as well, giving me two feminine
dimension dreams in Portugal to set me on the right foot for
Zurich.

(142)
*Someplace in the country, and something about a house in
a tree. Then I am with Dr. _____ (the older woman with
whom I worked so long in San Francisco) and she is cuddled
against my back for warmth while I tell her of an experience
with a great tree, magical perhaps, with many birds and other
creatures in its branches. She relates my experience to that of
a writer—George Eliot—and tells the title of a book, ____?____
Wycherley.*

(143)
*I am in a lovely large home, with a friend of mine, a woman
artist, and we are doing feminine things like dusting, making
beds, etc., to get ready for some event. She and I and an unknown woman, old and wise, are on a balcony looking at the
night sky and stars. My friend speaks to me some visionary or
prophetic sentence. I reply that is how I feel when I write fiction
—it takes hold of me and I go flashing into space. This is how it
is with the artist, I say, gesturing as I speak. I almost see something burst in the dark night sky.*

Both of these dreams presented Wise Woman helpers, both of them older, and in each case an almost magical event occurs: the great tree filled with creatures, and the night sky with stars and starbursts. The idea of writer and/or artists and the supranatural appears in both. On the other side of the psyche, however, was this dream:

(144)

I am watching violent scenes of David and Goliath being acted out in full medieval costume. Goliath hurls a huge metal ball at David when his back is turned, but doesn't hit him. I become very angry. Then, down a steep slope, at its bottom in a sort of canyon, I see a dark man pursuing two young women. He intends to hurt or to rape them. They are screaming and trying to escape but are not making it. I tell another man— possibly the David figure—and we rush to help the young women. The two men—the would-be rapist and David—begin fighting. I pick up a board and hit at the rapist. He pulls out a heavy revolver. I grab it, to his surprise, and point it at him. He defies me, saying to go ahead and shoot—as if he didn't believe I could or would. I don't know if I can.

So my demon, my Satan, my evil masculine dimension, was still there waiting to overcome the feminine.

It was good to arrive in Zurich from Portugal, from Portugal's warm spring sun to bitter cold and falling snow. It was very still, and the small but comfortable hotel so familiar to us was welcoming. I sat in my room that afternoon with mixed expectancy and fear, a desire to face myself more fully than I ever had and a fear of what would be revealed and my ability to deal with it creatively. What would my new analyst be like? I was beginning with a woman I did not know but who was highly recommended. (Dr. Frey was, and is, one of the most creative and helpful of all the analysts I have worked with, and it is at her urging that I am writing this book.)

We also arrived at Zurich in time for its great festival, *Secheleuten,* which heralds the coming of spring by burning Old Man Winter on a huge bonfire in the great square by the opera house, with mounted riders from each of the many well-known Guilds in Zurich riding full gallop around the burning. All of this is preceded by a parade with floral floats from all of the Guilds, and bands, lots of children marching, and flowers and noise. The night after the parade I had this dream:

(145)
Friends and I are living on a far planet. Two leave in a space-
ship for earth for a short trip. Just before they leave, a man
comes through a space port, wringing his hands, crying, saying
how he tried to prevent a spaceship accident but couldn't, so
several were killed. We are upset because one of us has to go.
But I thought that we take risks on earth also. Then we discover
that someone has been stealing our food in our house when
we are away. We decide to take them by surprise, sneak up a
stairway, and I am in the lead. Two women are at the table
eating. Seeing us, one comes brazenly towards me and says,
in effect, so what are you going to do? I am furious and lunge
at her, half-waking myself up in my anger. (I don't know where
it came out.) Then a friend and I want to go somewhere on the
surface of this planet. I am aware of some very strange crea-
tures, half plant and half animal, growing out of the earth,
turning this way and that like snakes or plants to know what
is going on. Somehow I learn that the name of this planet is
Interieure, *or* Dongeon, *or perhaps* Dongeon Interieure.

[*Later in the night*] *A land sled is coming fast down slopes,*
with men guiding it; it slithers around a curve and stops sud-
denly at the edge of a cliff. The leader complains of not enough
glassy sand all the way. They were bringing something of mine
to me.

Although this dream fascinated me, it also made me uneasy for reasons I could not at that time explain. The far planet felt to be a microcosm, the world egg, the spiritual-Self world, cosmos and center with windows out, whereas the earth would be the physical-self world of outer reality. From its name, the planet seemed to be inside, interior, a confinement of some kind. The little snake-like creatures felt related to the phoenix, or to the salamander of alchemy which can live through the fire. They were earthy and yet had the ability to keep track of what was happening. The Dongeon aspect of the planet related to problems in my Eighth and Twelfth houses of the zodiac—both houses

related to prisons or hospitals or confinements and thus both
represented the need for much inwardness. The land sled running
on sand I related to the alchemical stage that follows the "watery"
and unconscious one—where sand is called the "pure substance
of the Stone," the regenerated earth. The women stealing food
represented the unconscious feminine dimension negativities
that robbed me of my inner substance. Also, it seemed clear that
this Interieure Dongeon was exactly where I needed to live for
the next months as I entered into a new stage of my journey with
a new helper.

Liliane Frey-Rohn is soft-spoken, direct, with eyes that sparkle
and dance even when she speaks harsh truths. She brings the best
of the Swiss and the best of the French to all that she does. Her
way to the inner world has been compensatory to mine from the
beginning—her intuition meshes with my sensation richly.

After I told her about my psychic upheavals and demonic
male figures, she said, "You are facing the devil of your life now.
He is too metallic and yet he holds a great value. He must be met,
grappled with, transformed—but not killed."

So we went far back in time to my early Terrible Dream (see
Chapter I). She felt I had carried the family's shadow, not mine,
and probably had suffered deeply from my mother's darkness
which had been so repressed. The winged batman (dream (0),
Chapter I) seemed related to Mercury, an ambivalent being, which
had taken me into the intellect too much but which did have real
spiritual values to be discovered.

The dream of the man abusing the horse (131) showed how
my animus abused all earthy things—and because I was earthy
abused my very nature. The mother archetype had been poisoned
so that neither I (with my allergies) nor part of my masculine
dimension that had been poisoned (137) could deal with it. Now
it had to be rediscovered, helped to be actively concerned for
the self's well-being.

We discussed at length the dream (141) about the book, *The
Plunder of Time,* by Satan. Perhaps, she felt, my anxieties and
fears about time, its passing, and its terrors, were because I was
split between activity (which I related to my mother and thus

judged as good) and passivity (which I related to my father and
thus judged as bad). She kept stressing that I carried some deep
and repressed shadow-darkness *of the family*—of the Christian
Science and fundamentalist Methodist attitudes that the body
and matter, in general, were bad and to be held in close check.
Thus I could not see the dead-Hell-Devil dream and the batman
dream as anything but evil, which left me isolated and haunted.
Dr. Frey quoted a statement from alchemy about the Devil: "a
process that begins with evil and ends with good."

Then came the first dream of this part of the Journey, especially
chosen by whatever powers choose just the right thing at the
right time in order to push us into the unwelcome places we need
to enter.

(146)
*I am in a strange city, sitting in a square overlooking the city.
It is near water—river, lake, sea(?). There is a row of old stone
seats with people sitting in them. I sit across from this row. A
young black girl is in the second seat of the row, right across
from me. The first seat is covered with small brown turds,
probably animal rather than human. The girl and I begin to
talk. I seem to ask her to do something—not for me, but because
it will mean something perhaps to her. She says she will if
someone will smear these feces around. I think about doing
it, but very reluctantly. Finally I put out my right hand on
which I am wearing Harry's engagement ring, and I mash the
feces down and smear them around on the stone. When I have
them well-smeared—the girl watching me silently—I stop and
turn to her. She smiles, and says something about our earlier
conversation. Is she willing now? I don't remember if she does
anything. I bang my hand against the bench base to get some
of the feces off, then say I must wash so as not to spread infection. Hand and ring are sticky with feces. To find a place to
wash I make my way around pools of water and wet stones, as
if water had risen and flooded here. I wash hands and ring and
return to the girl, saying, "I guess we get a lot of poison every
day anyway." Then later, perhaps in the same city, I am wandering in less built-up areas where there are sloping fields and
open space. A woman tells me a man is giving flu shots. I meet*

him on a path. He is big, smiling warmly, dressed in clerical black as if a rabbi or a priest, and his clothes and hair seem covered with small seeds, as if he had been rolling on a threshing floor. He is carrying a hypodermic syringe. I say something about having had a flu shot. Very friendly, he replies to the effect that even so what he has will protect me. (I connected him, even in the dream, with Silenus.)

As soon as I wakened I began putting my associations into the dream. The stone seats reminded me of Demeter's seat at Eleusis —of cosmic proportions, hewn of native stone—and of the royal thrones at Cnossos. In my sketch of the seats I found I had five in one row, with my seat opposite the first of the five, the one with the feces. And five is both the number of the human, and the *quintaessentia,* the essence. My ring from Harry, which I usually wear on my left hand, was actually made from his mother's engagement ring and my mother's wedding ring, so the Mothers are here for certain. Silenus is the wise old god who stands behind Dionysus and Ariadne in the fresco at the Villa of Mysteries, Pompeii.

As Dr. Frey and I talked during my next hour, we saw it was a turning point dream. The darkness here was so different from the demonic dreams. Here it was the darkness of the black girl— the forgotten, the second-class, the ignored (but also proud enough to want freedom) and the one who can help if ego is willing to pay the price. And the price, for an ego that had hidden for years behind goodness and propriety, is high. It is an act of heroism to get involved in the filth and poison of the animal nature—something my ego had cut off from, denied, shunned, even though my period of drinking and carousing had lived out of it but irresponsibly and unconsciously. Now it had to be very conscious, very deliberate. The ring related my action to the Mothers, and my right hand related my action to full consciousness.

The man in black was spirit, as rabbi or priest, and he was nature, as Silenus. He was also somewhat Oriental, resembling the Hotei statues of China. His syringe seemed to contain a protection —perhaps quietness, meditation, humor—from the infections of our time. The roundness of his face had impressed me. We won-

dered if this could be symbolic of the opposite of the round ball
thrown so viciously by Goliath (144). This dream, and the work
with it, led me within the week into a long and central active
imagination.

The next dream furnished further insights, both about how the
animus of the woman can be split apart and how I really needed
to take on the small, lost animus neglected by my mother.

(147)

I had planned a huge Guild affair with a Zurich Jungian as
speaker, but others are delaying the start by a long and trivial
meeting in another place. I am angry at those who cause the
delay. When I reach the lecture hall things still are not ready,
and the planners are chatting. Again I am angry, and say
that the guest is a fine lecturer, has much to give, and then I
make the introduction. She tells a fairy tale, and acts it as she
tells it, looking into mirrors, gesturing, tiptoeing about, all with
great verve and delight, enjoying herself like a puckish child.

Then (later in night) I see some toddler crawling on a ledge
outside of the room where I am. He could fall, could land in the
street, and is in danger. I go to him and ask him why he is
there. He says, "Because I'm lonely." (He was actually too small
to have said this.) So I lift him to take him in, feel his little
naked body soft and warm, and he suddenly urinates all over
the ledge. I put him inside, hoping he hasn't wet my clothes.

This night pointed up to me how concerned I was about all
things being in order, including my feelings, which must never
be disorderly.

When Dr. Frey and I came to the place where I hoped the
little boy hadn't wet my clothes, she asked with a smile, "Why
shouldn't he have?" And despite my fussing at the lecture planners so that everything would proceed correctly, the lecturer
behaved like the delighted and delightful child, combining logos
and pixie, teaching and play. I was beginning to see what "deadly
serious" meant, and that I was, too often. The baby boy was sort
of an orphan, and perhaps I was being asked to be his mother, to
move him from loneliness to love.

Dr. Frey pointed out that often women have two animus

parts—one that they live out quite well and one that has been caught in the mother. The second one tends to be orphaned and lonely. So it was for me. Now he is for me to care for.

We returned to the dream of the planet, Dongeon Interieure (145). At times the work must be tackled head on—and Dr. Frey felt the planet dream asked that. This Interieure Dongeon is really my place, my ground, related to my horoscope, and probably related to creativity which had been held down for years. The boy baby was another statement of creativity potential needing me to look after it, work with it, be concerned about it. These two dreams of the baby and the Dongeon have remained centrally meaningful since that time. Dongeon is the place from which my writing and my paintings come, a place in which I can live happily for long days at a time.

From the dream of Interieure Dongeon until the final dream in Europe in 1969, Dr. Frey and I worked with inner material that was packed with meaning. I found it difficult to leave this deep inward work and return to the daily world of outer work, friends, seminars, patients, and housekeeping. For a person of my temperament it is like changing the car I am driving from a stickshift VW to an automatic transmission. It takes a bit of practice before I feel at home. This time the transition seemed more difficult than ever, despite the fact that all was going well when I left Europe and seemed to be going well in the summer seminars that followed. I believe now, as I go back over it, I had not allowed enough time in quietness to absorb all the rich inner and outer growings from Europe. This trip was especially so because of the frontal attack on my inner demon. He needed longer to die, that is certain, and because that time was not given he erupted in a totally unexpected way.

My first dream after returning home was that one of my friends had tuberculosis and had to go for a rest cure to a Swiss mountain sanitarium. I wrote about it:

Journal

This is saying that my first month here is dangerous to me, that the spirit would overextend itself and not stay related to the

Swiss introvertedness, that I must listen to body sensation warnings, be alone and inward and on the earth as much as possible,
be vigilant and aware, keep the light touch. My intuitive and
feeling shadow could quickly get a disease if my negative devil
gets in there.

Two nights later I dreamed almost the same dream, and again
understood it as I had the first. But I did not listen. I kept on
having helpful dreams.

(148)
*I am in Europe with a Hindu family. The man gives me a
strange gnarled root, very aromatic,* to hold and smell. *It has*
curative *powers.*

(149)
Of a small fledgling bird in a pose that was so asleep *as to
be like hibernation. When I gently tried to stroke it, some caked
mud came away from its eyes but the* eyes stayed shut *and its
tiny breast moved only a very little with its breathing. I learned
that it was* to be kept and cared for *and raised by a bantam hen,*
when it was time.

(150)
*I am with a warm, alive, loving, older woman, a nun. She is
very relaxed as we talk. I say that she, and other nuns like her,
carry the role of the* meaningful, introverted, feminine, religious
life for others. She agrees, with a smile.

(151)
*In a gathering where Jung is to speak. I am with him behind
the scenes and we talk personally. He is small, old, wrinkled,
gentle, humorous, like one of the very old Navajo gods (Talking
God or Fire God). He is asking me about me personally. The
meeting is late starting because of our personal talk. Later on
a woman comes in to address the group. She has had some very
important spiritual initiation and as a mark of that she has
the lower half of her face painted with red clay. Finally I come
to some gathering with only my underclothes on. People are
shocked but I am not embarrassed or guilty.*

The inner dreamer spoke clearly: I needed to remain rooted,
related to the curative earth powers. The small new life was all

right, but I needed to let it stay quiescent until it was time for it
to fly. The introverted and quiet way was what I needed. I needed
the personal, even if the impersonal had to wait. I was not yet
garbed in a proper persona for the world. These messages I should
have heard. My physical body heard them. The arthritis wors-
ened, especially in my left leg, developing slowly into sciatica.
I tried to ignore it. The summer was exciting with many new
people in seminars, and I was enjoying it all, finding the work
more rewarding than ever before.

Finally I got this message:

(152)
*The sentence was: "Wars and blisters in the street find (define)
young children."*

Journal

Violence, conflict, upheaval, fires that burn up the usual ways—
these things lead to a discovery of new growth coming. As if the
"children" in me had been hidden until the chaos reveals their
presence. I am filled with quiet war! I don't understand it yet.
It is irrational, nonverbal, confusing, but not fearful. Some new
stance is perhaps emerging. Also my insistent "define" when I
know the word was "find" must mean that the inner upheaval
does delineate, bring out, the new life direction.

The next day I was expected to lead a group of new people on
a "blind" walk around the grounds—that is, I walked backward
holding the hand of the first person in the line so I was leading
all of the line, linked hand-to-hand, with their eyes closed so that
they could experience all of the senses. The walk went off well,
but next morning I could hardly stand because of severe pain
down my left leg. However, I went on with my usual work for
about a week. Then this dream came:

(153)
*An old old woman has died, and her funeral procession is
being held. Led by an old man as the minister-priest, the procession approaches the church. The old lady is seated as if
behind a high desk, her head upright, her chin resting on the
desk, her face very wrinkled (like a mask), a strong and resolute*

aged face. She wore the cap of early Flemish times with a wide starched ruff framing it and her dead face. I felt she was an ancestor of mine.

This was the funeral of my ancestral pattern of courage, of chin up, be resolute, never lie down on a job, accomplish, succeed. The negative masculine dimension had infected my female forebears this way, I believe.

A few days later the doctor ordered me to bed. I was first in bed at home, and then at the hospital in traction, for six weeks. Then I had spinal surgery to remove a ruptured spinal disc, another hospital stay, and several weeks of recovery.

This was a long, rich, learning time. Forced to be quiet, to do nothing, to let my inner world in all its dimensions flow, I came to terms with the demon of my life in a more thorough way than I could ever have done otherwise. He was so reduced in size that he has never since been able to threaten to topple me. The caring of friends was overwhelming—and at times like this friends express their feelings honestly and directly. Once more, during this period, I also had to learn (again) that the so-called irrational mode would instruct me about what to do. Some of my dreams came to help me, clearly taking the side of new life to come; others were warnings, reminders to be more careful.

I went with friends to Palm Springs for a period of relaxation. I took time for myself. My inner life began to change, giving me scenes of small beasts and joyful play, of wonderful cathedrals in mandala arrangements, of big houses filled with warm people who could care for orphaned children, and many wanderings in labyrinthine cities under the earth. I spent some time with an old friend in Carmel. I had several experiences of feeling that people who were dead were standing beside me as I wakened, or just before I went to sleep. I spent as much time as I could at our seminar place in northern California, with long and leisurely hours in my cabin reading or writing, or gathering back my physical strength by walking in the woods and watching the birds.

At Eastertime we went to Santa Fe, New Mexico, to visit the always colorful Indian country—its tinted deserts, its long and delicately contoured mountains, its native people with their faces weatherworn and wise, its scattered flocks of sheep, its ancient ruins. I never tire of this land. I was born not too far from it— in Colorado—and somehow it is imbedded in my very structure, physical and psychic.

Easter was ushered in by this dream:

(154)
I find an old box containing black and white photographs that I have taken of Dr. and Mrs. Jung, Toni Wolff, Linda Fierz, and others, all elegantly dressed and coming down a great staircase as at an opera or a reception.

Also there were photos from a place called Herculeum or Heraculeum, with special scenes of the labors of Herakles. These had been either painted scenes or scenes in relief, but each was like a rosette or medallion, and I had cut them out that way.

All of these were Zurich people who had died. I felt that I was letting the dead past go but remembering that each of them had been dedicated, working at selfhood, courageous, and each had been helpful in my becoming. So the task being stated was the "labors of Herakles," the way in which I needed to go, remembering also Kazantzakis and his grave in Heraklion, Crete, and his passion for self-knowing and God-seeking, for the death-rebirth journey.

XI

Death-Rebirth Cycles (May 1970–August 1971)

The seasons moved toward Christmas 1970, when I would be sixty years old. At least two-thirds of my life was already gone. As I looked over this last year of my fifties, I asked myself what its major learnings were. This is how I set them out:

1. With thirty dreams of a variety of labyrinthine confusions, mess, disorder, lostness, wandering, wrong people, doing other people's jobs—it is certain that I have been sent into a new level of the alchemical *nigredo*.

2. With seven dreams of lost, abused, sick, dying, burned, and dead animals, it seems clear that my instinctual side was crying for help. In most cases, help came.

3. R_____'s death has been a deep death-rebirth symbol to me in many ways.

4. A specifically religious element has run through the year's dreams—with churches, monasteries, convents appearing from time to time, as well as many sentences about religious attitudes, ways to pray, about the nature of God.

5. Three important "hiding" dreams have come: putting jewels in clay balls for young people; the young artist woman

hiding from all but me; and the St. George Statue with the young life inside. All of these are telling me clearly that the treasure is inside, is hidden and must be hidden until the old ego images are shattered. What has worked before will work no more. The new is hidden, shy, fragile, young, jewel-like, and must be cared for.

Outwardly this last year of my fifties had held moving, exciting new adventures. My relationship with my two closest friends had matured as we worked at it under any and all circumstances. We had taken holidays away from work. We had given seminars in California, other states, Canada. Our leadership training program for the Guild was growing, and we could begin to let some of the younger leaders take responsibility. Illness and death had added some dark colors, but the bright colors were always there.

With three dear friends I had gone to the threshold of death, had seen them leave with that final exhalation that takes them where I have never been. Each experience—of being with them during their final days and hours and minutes, of seeing them struggle with the Other and work desperately and often joyously with the Other to learn what was to be learned—filled me with anguish, awe, sorrow, and a new sense of what life is about. They showed the willingness and courage to look into those Eyes straight on, helping me see that death and birth stand together, hand in hand.

After the death and funeral of one woman friend, I had many dreams of her in life and in death, with over and again a sense of rebirth, or her being present. This shared experience opened new vistas of what needed to be reborn in me. Her strangely vibrant stillness—one of her most unique characteristics—was a rich symbol for many others as well as for me. The night after we had placed her ashes at the base of a great oak tree, I dreamed that some woman used the Tarot cards and turned up the card of Death. Then the dream went on:

(155)
Many people are arriving at some gathering. There is a sense of gaiety and joy. First I read aloud a few lines from a child's

*play that we all knew and loved. There was a wonderful and
wildly dressed and funny and very lovable woman there, a new
friend of mine, an actress as well as some sort of therapist with
groups. She and I discuss therapies. A zany man friend comes
and we play clown for a few minutes. Then a small, gypsy-type
man enters with a nanny goat and an adorable kid. The kid
comes to me and nuzzles me lovingly. I wish it were mine. The
actress-therapist says she had one once and loved it. "And when
they grow old," she tells me, "they must have a special rug on
which to die." This touched me deeply.*

Two nights later I had a dream which still stands out as one of
the most important ones of my life. Somehow I feel it is connected with this dream about the kid.

(156)
*I am in a big house with people coming and going. Mostly I
am with a young woman in her 20's whom I have recently met.
She is shy and, I learn later, not at all well. She has angina,
plus other rheumatic and bodily diseases. She is also a painter,
and there are several fantastically beautiful paintings in her
rooms, one of a person looking up into an apocalyptic sky in
which some sort of rocket or atom blast has just been released.
At some point she gives me a beautiful ancient Chinese figure
of an old wise man, not unlike the Bodhidarma figures, with
long robes and a beard. It is made of cloth, woven cloth, and is
to be worn. It is about a foot high. Other people come to visit
me suddenly—some I have known in the past, some current
friends. The young woman disappears. Later I find that she has
hidden under a couch in her room when they were there because
she is afraid that I don't love her and will talk about her or
betray her. I assure her that none of this is true—talking with
her as she lies in bed because of her health.*

Here was a real clue to much of my sense of loneliness, of wandering in an alien world, of not feeling I belonged. She was the
girl I had lost in my twenties, a girl painfully shy and not too
strong physically. I had kept her hidden, shut away, ignored, in
the big house where "things get done." She was my artist side,
with apocalyptic visions and the seeress's wisdom. Now I had
to love her, to keep her very close to my heart. Behind her, I

came to see, was the nanny goat and the little kid. The kid was what she could be if I found her and cared for her. She could also transcend the lower animals, offering the gifts and the struggles of the artist and the artist's visions, all of which were slowly coming alive in me. I saw why it had taken so long for my creativity to get free. A series of dreams began which affirmed what was going on.

(157)
Just before waking I saw a scene of a small village, with a sense of green and brown buildings, much white snow, and a large, pinkish-red horse standing in a yard. He was very big, like a work horse, and beautiful to see. I did not want to wake up, but just to stare at him.

(158)
I wakened with a vision of an enormous and beautiful snake coiled on some rise or pedestal. It was olive green and terra cotta in a lovely pattern.

These dreams were a vocal Yes! Something strong and colorful and of the energic earth was being manifest. Another dream was filled with hidden healthy laughter.

(159)
I was in a house I didn't know, except that we, or I, seemed to be living there, or moving into it. I came into one room and found, amid the general disorder, a big and old chest. Inside the chest I found a very old and wonderfully carved wood piece. It was of St. George, but in a most unusual position. His body was bent forward, his head drooping (like the famous statue and painting of the American Indian chieftain in defeat, known as "The End of the Trail").

Then I could see inside this figure, and there were tiny figures of children, and perhaps of animals or other living things. All of this seemed to have to do with Christmas.

I have never been very taken by St. George in his proud dragon-slaying, a bit inflated on his great horse and with his princess helper. But *my* St. George is a rather sad hero and seems in fact to be at the end of the trail. This *defeated* conqueror is the cradle for the nest of tiny living beings, and all somehow related to the

new birth, to Christmas! What a wonderful joke on the negative
animus who had worked so long and so hard to be heroic and
conquering!

In a short period, between Thanksgiving and Christmas, I had
five dreams of the friend who had died in July—rich and revealing dreams, but always with a sense of mystery. In one she was
telling me about some new paintings she was doing, but she
seemed to talk in a language I did not understand. One dream,
a strange mixture of chaos and joy, tried to encompass all that
was going on:

(160)
*In a big house with many people trying to prepare for the
Day of the Dead ritual, except that it also seems to involve
preparing for Christmas. There is a great lack of order, with
people going in all directions. I seem to be working at Christmas
things—books, Advent wreaths, parts of a manger scene, with
greens everywhere, and a tree. Trash of various kinds covers
the floors and I'm trying to clean it up.*

And just a few days before Christmas I dreamed again of the dead
friend:

(161)
*Suddenly R_____ appears, in some vehicle from which I
drew her out with joy. She greets all three of us with an embrace.
She is casually dressed, smiling, and says that she has had to
drop out of everything, to get away, to find herself. I seem to be
telling her things to help her to get back—although I feel that
she really doesn't want any help. She is loving and happy but
wants to be just what she is, where she is.*

This dream seemed related to the frightened artist in dream (156),
who also had to be just what she was until I found her and
listened to her.

We spent Christmas in Mexico, with a hot sun, the babble and
squeal of playing children on holiday, firecrackers resounding
against walls, women going to market, church bells ringing. I felt
that Mexico—and Taxco more than most places I've been—
resembled the Holy Land, especially Bethlehem. Noise, dirt,
squalor, and touching tenderness all mixed together.

I awakened ill and weak on Christmas Eve, my year nearing its end in real darkness of body and soul. I was swamped by the terrible draining conflicts of the humanness of people, including my own.

In his book *Alchemical Studies,* Dr. Jung writes:

> . . . The divine process of change manifests itself to our human understanding . . . as punishment, death, and transfiguration . . .
>
> We must be able to let things happen in the psyche. For us, this is an art of which most people know nothing. Consciousness is forever interfering, helping, correcting, and negating, never letting the psychic processes grow in peace. It would be simple enough, if only simplicity were not the most difficult of all things.

On Christmas night this divine process of change became an almost unendurable suffering for me. Then, leaving the hotel next morning we walked into the heartbreak of youthful death—a silent procession of villagers, with six young men bearing the white casket of a young friend on their backs, followed by weeping women and dark-eyed solemn men. After the requiem mass in the small church, the silent procession started out again toward some distant cemetery. It was almost too much to bear. It was my death, everyman's death, the great passing beyond which no man knows. Some of me died, too, and I wept.

I believe that God—the Nothing wanting to become Something —is at work in every moment of a life. It doesn't matter that mostly we do not tune in on that Nothing, or that we prevent it from becoming Something. I believe that in every conscious choice I make, especially those in which there is pain and sacrifice and discipline and effort and love, that precisely there God is situational, at work in the world in which I live and in which I affect other people.

This is my history, granted that I do not do well by it most of the time. But I believe God is there in history—my history, the world's history—needing me (us) to make creative choices.

Such meaning regarding choices conveys itself in different ways to different people. It pressed me with a great urgency of the true nature of death and rebirth for the last third of my life.

I began 1971 with a dream that offered the option of choosing to die in order to be reborn. When I wakened from it, I lay for a long time as though it were true, feeling deep inside that it had to do not only with inner rebirth but with some kind of outer return as well.

The year moved quickly in 1971. Seminars were rich. *A Magic Dwells* was on the booklists; *Joseph's Son* was at the printers. The 1971 spring at my cabin gave me the loveliness of lilacs, white locust blossoms, orchards bright and shining, happy cats, nesting birds, all the paraphernalia of the season.

Easter week, however, had its own plans, obviously made by Someone else. I was pushed into bed again by arthritis. Being ill and in bed with pain is a trying but rewarding way to learn what one needs. I lay in my bed in my cabin for the greater part of Easter week, looking out at my trees, enjoying occasional visitors and meal-bringers.

I learned that the more I could sustain creative aloneness, keep myself down, quiet, caring for a difficult body with love, the more joy I had with the people for whom I cared. I became clearer with myself. Being alone, I found, kept me from leaning or demanding or trying to please. It forced me to let go of the little things I usually fuss about. It pushed me into a place of solitude and more meditation and stillness.

Easter Sunday I went into the hospital. Later in the day when I opened a book of passages from various sources, I saw these words:

> Save me, O God, for the waters have come in, even unto my soul. (Psalm 69)

> When shall I enjoy true freedom, untrammeled and untroubled in mind and body? (Thomas à Kempis)

Matters do seem to fall into place whenever I get out of the way. I looked around my antiseptic room and saw three joyful red tulips, three opening dogwood blossoms, one talisman rose, a silly yellow rabbit with a hula skirt, and a basket of white roses giving the very best of the last they had to give. Under them was a skewed white horse, a crystal squirrel against a stained glass window, and a bright pink horse just above Middle Earth. "God bless," I said aloud. "Let me rest and learn."

With my years of psychological and religious training and work, I knew a great deal about the things of darkness. But that experience in the hospital of having them come, unbidden, with voices of their own, telling me things newly and freshly, albeit not always enjoyably, was one I would not have given up. It was a strange and chaotic time, coming suddenly and unexpectedly, with confusion, pain, and lots of loving support. Out of it, I wrestled with despair, priorities, where my life was going, what I needed to do.

There were bright moments also, as when I found this line written by a Greek: ". . . the great home of the air-walking winds." This line ran in and through me at odd moments for days, each time bringing with it a sense of soaring, of mystery unfathomed and of joy.

The day after I came home from the hospital, this dream:

(162)
Someone presented me with a conundrum, printed on long paper. They thought I couldn't solve it, but it seems that I did. It read: "The trick is you must always tell the honest particulate unique truth, but so that it must have the full reality of the generalized."

This, then, was the task being set me by this life crisis.

In September, at the end of a summer of seminars, I moved back again into work on my own death-rebirth journey, in Zurich.

XII

Rending and Sewing (September 1971–January 1972)

Journal

[September 1971] Switzerland again. Today, once more, I start into the depths of myself with my loving guide. I approach this first hour as a virgin and a harlot. Pure openness, yet filled with the sins and fears of a lifetime. It is the beginning of a new exploration. I pray that the great inscrutable Presence will surround me and lead me. May I go how I must go, so what I love may be free and overflowing. I've no notion where to begin—with what or whom—but I know that all levels, from the worst to the best, must be enfolded.

I knew that I needed to give up everything for the sake of a new step in my growth—needed to give up being needed, being creative, being right, being busy. On the whole my outer world had been going well, with the exception of relationships, always my *bête noir*. Too many of my relationships suffered from my negative animus, and I suffered from it as well. This was why, I believe, I had this dream of death.

(163)
I was in some inner rooms with a group of people. The main

object of our being there was to prepare to die and to choose when to have the injection that would bring death. Dr. J_____ (a dear older woman physician who had died some years before) was administering the injections. She was very happy and filled with joy. She herself had died and returned. Any of us who so chose could also die and return. Two young girls were there, dressed in bright orange colors, telling of their happiness since they had done this. Now, they said, they could just be with people lovingly and not be troubled. There were others talking of their return, also with joy. I was getting ready to have my injection. Before anyone could have it they had to let go of everything in their lives—possessions, attitudes, etc. A man physician was helping Dr. J_____, and he gave me a list and asked what would be hardest for me to let go of. I said, breaking into tears, that it would be those I loved. Somewhere I was also asked what I most wanted to bring back with me and I answered, again in tears, "LOVE"! I held a little tin box that contained the very last remnants of my possessions, emptied it, and very slowly closed it. Some friends were there with me. Also some men who had come back were preparing a sort of clown mime show.

The entire dream was full of deep emotion. I can still feel it. It was very real. I felt that it had to do not only with inner rebirth but with some kind of outer return and rebirth as well. It did not have a nightmare quality, but depth of a kind I had known only rarely in my dreams. Of course, it became the center of my analytic work this time with Dr. Frey. Other themes also presented themselves—of a kind different than before, thus also giving us strong clues. Here are a few:

(164)
I am being prepared, and preparing, to join an order—one which although not cloistered is "in the world but not of it" entirely. One nun is giving me the clothes I am to wear for the joining. There is a full length, pale, lacy petticoat, then a lovely deep rose satin full length robe, and finally a full length black habit, rich and pleated and not traditional. There is much wandering about in buildings, laying out the clothes, trying to find a place to dress. I pass the great church where I feel I will be taken into the order. It seems festive, maybe with gifts.

*One nun tells me that sometimes I can wear the rose satin as a
gown. Then I am walking on a street, as in a medieval city.
I am fully robed, with the black robe on the outside, wearing
old and worn walking shoes. I feel quiet, dignified, proud,
and very alone.*

(165)
*One of my close friends announced that she had married. She
was very casual, seeming not to consider the total change of
life style it would be for everyone involved. Then I was wandering about in a strange city not being able to find where I lived.*

(166)
*A terrible man with gasoline and a gun to explode it—but
the bullet did not spark the gasoline so he put all of it in his
mouth and spewed it into someplace which was hot. Flames
burst forth, engulfed him and burned him to death. I could hear
flesh crackle and see him disintegrate. I ran. I found someone,
told them what had happened and that I couldn't stay near.*

(167)
*My doctor told me that she had discovered that I had some
brain damage as well as a kidney malfunction. They were
caused by childhood accidents.*

(168)
*(I wakened talking aloud, wrote the words down, and then
recalled a dream.)*

> *your tiny feet click*
> *ahead of me*
> *hunting for food in bowls*
> *I do not have*
> *I must get some for you*
> *you are hungry and alone*
> *as I am*
> *and I love you*
> *as I stroke your feathers.*

*(dream) I was a clown, a fool, a wanderer, dressed in ragged
clothes and worn shoes with holes in them. I didn't know where
I was going. I saw a half-grown chick wandering alone near
me, pecking here and there for food. I realized it was hungry
and alone, and that I very much wanted to care for it because
I needed something to love and to protect. I stroked its scrawny*

feathers. I also resolved to find a bowl of some sort so that I could give it food and drink. I suddenly realized that I would beg or steal golden corn for my chick.

Surely there's no doubt that these dreams—and others like them—indicated a rending apart of old adaptations. So Dr. Frey and I reviewed the old adaptations fully and painfully, which helped me see that all that goes on in a life (even the wrong things) is not wasted. What I had already struggled through in the long years until now had enriched and filled out the writing and teaching that I was doing. The retrospective look helps, even if it is painful. It is necessary from time to time if the growth of the deeper Self is involved.

It was time for me to be choosing my death (163) and to become a nun (164) or a wandering fool with a half-starved chick for a comrade. The danger of my destructive animus was never more clearly or nightmarishly put than in dream (166). In one sense the only way he can be avoided or outwitted is by my being a nun or a fool, in one way or another. Dreams (165) and (167) speak, at the personal level, of new ways being found, and of seeing shortcomings as related to childhood wounds and thus as not entirely my fault but just in the nature of things.

My journal serves to bring the immediacy of experience:

Journal

Dr. Frey and I have just been walking through the inner world of dreams I've had during the two years since I was last here in Switzerland. So many warned me—i.e., a friend had tuberculosis and needed rest in Swiss mountains; so many had symbols of earth and water, i.e., a mandrake root, an elephant, a bird not yet ready to hatch, a nun, a bemused artist. I see how deeply I needed to let go of the spirit drive, the too-muchness of demands, after we came here two years ago. One should always be on guard against returns, because they so quickly impose a strain on newly healed wounds. My sense of humor can often aid me in seeing the dangers, because it comes closer to expressing real feelings. Also, my body tells me, either of itself or in dreams, when matters are diseased. I must let the nun, warm, alive, quiet, be related to before I can serve outwardly. I must let the bemused artist stay bemused as long as he must.

There were a goodly number of dreams about fun, toys, games, dances. Perhaps the new mandala for me is more related to Shiva's dance of death and rebirth as "play." Dr. Frey said she felt life had laid heavy burdens on me for small sins, as if I were being shaped into an "advanced soul." My mind backs away from such ideas. My heart wonders. As we looked at a painting I had done, naming it "Lonesome Valley," we talked of St. John of the Cross, his dark night lighted only by the flame of love in his heart, and we saw how relevant to all this is the scene in my novel, *Knee-Deep in Thunder,* when the young girl must enter the cave of death to find her own light.

I feel more and more alone as I get older, especially when I am doing inner work, because through this work I am increasingly aware of my absolute uniqueness—an almost incommunicable uniqueness. Love becomes more rich but more wordless.

There is a realization that all are alike at the source. I feel this intensely these days.

As often as possible when I am in Switzerland, I go to Einsiedeln, the place of the Black Virgin. I went there in 1971 on my mother's birthday. She was a year and a half younger when she died than I was on that day. She died of a driving will and repressed and/or distorted feelings—very like the negative animus I was battling with. Something important happened that day at Einsiedeln.

Journal

Sunday morning at Einsiedeln. Too many people are with the Black Virgin, so I have come the more solitary way of the stations of the cross, winding up through a forested path, past the brown mares with their wonderfully arched necks and eager eyes. Now I stand within a few feet of the thirteenth station—the Pieta— closer than I have ever been. I see that her eyes are looking, not at the dead Jesus, but at me. At me and through me, holding me hypnotized with the inevitable sorrow of the world and the flesh. And yet there is acceptance in her far-seeing gaze. "Death and Birth are one," the eyes seem to say. "God is with me now as on that first occasion. The Holy Spirit comes as it will. I see into all eyes, those windows of the heart, and I feel with them. With you among others. All are born, suffer, die—and go on. I am the Mother of all."

So as I groped toward a deepened sense of meaning and an expansion of truth, the natural beauty of this precariously tidy country gave me space to breathe in. Here I could find, perhaps because there is so little that could prevent me from hiding, an earth to walk on and chunks of numinosity to move me. During this period I also gave a seminar at the mountain home of one of Jung's daughters, on an American Indian myth. It was exciting to see a group of Swiss responding to our folklore. And I too responded—with this call to Changing Woman, central deity of the Navajo.

Journal

Changing Woman! Lovely child of joyous laughter, of eggs and nests and birds, of vibrant blue gentians and snow-striped heights, please be alive in my heart. I long to be aware of You as You move through me, as You are moving me, as I move in You. Help me to be more of the time with You on Your rainbowed mountain. Help me also to bring more of You and Your vital fullness into my surroundings—more excitement and loving blossoming, more spiritual song, more expressiveness.

I used this unlikely combination of a Black Virgin and Changing Woman of the Navajo Indians to push back the Death Demon animus that had clung to me, haunted me, so long. In analytic sessions we reviewed the feminine dimension in my life. My mother had had to fall back on her competent and driving animus masculine dimension and to abandon her natural feelings during the long harsh depression years. Caught in the same pattern, I moved in with a roommate who gave me undifferentiated feelings, and helped me over all sorts of obstacles, but who demanded of me that I be structured and clear thinking.

Unconscious, lost, and egocentric, I made the trade. I did this in other relationships, both with men and women, so that by the time I was thirty my survival equation was: to be needed = to be loved. Except with Harry. He could usually outthink me, and what he needed from me was to let him love me. And, of course, he hoped that I loved him. I did. But my Death Demon drove me, over and over, with a deadly fire, doing, doing, doing, never feeling I was doing enough.

As we worked with these things, I saw that all of the hospital-
izations had, in one sense, been messages from the feminine
dimension that I needed to let go, give over, stop.

Dr. Frey said, "Lie on the grass and be. Be irrational. You have
been too bound. You must unbind."

We decided at this point to review my natal horoscope that
Jung's daughter, Gret Baumann-Jung, had done some years before
(see Chapter VI). As we went into it, we saw that Uranus, creative,
irrational, the major ruler of my horoscope, and Mercury, the
planet of knowing, being both in the house of prison, meant that
from the first of my life I had to descend, one way or another,
to the depths of the archetypal unconscious to survive. And
each time the house of prison is brought into centrality (about
every thirty years from the year of birth) there are bound to be
upheavals, changes, conflicts, before a new level can be reached.

Now, in my sixtieth year, this was once more happening.
Uranus, a planet which can be sudden, creative and brutal, was
in bad aspects with Neptune, ruler of the seas of the unconscious.
So this was one way of describing why I had been feeling so
intense about some new direction being at hand. Or needing
to be found. Also Mars (fiery, youthful, driving) was badly
aspected to Saturn (second ruler of my horoscope, orderly, disciplined, repressive). And both of these planets were badly
aspected to my Aquarius rising sign. So I began to feel a great
sympathy for Aquarius (revolutionary, free, impulsive, independent) being so continuously torn between the fire of Mars and
the cold of Saturn. I saw how I so often could be caught in the
demonic drivenness of Mars' hyperactivity, and then shortly after
could be equally caught in the demonically repressive "No!"
of Saturn.

As for my feelings, my natal Moon was in the Eighth house of
sacrifice and was also badly aspected to Neptune. This described
clearly my great misuse of my feelings. Pluto, planet of the underworld, is in the house of home and my family—and in Gemini.
Certainly feelings and instincts had been somehow made dark
and poisonous in my family background, as witness dream (21),
of the ancestors and "Murder! Murder!" coming out of the earth

beside the ancestral home.

On the whole, as Dr. Frey said with a smile, my horoscope is a very difficult one—as was Dr. Jung's and hers, as well as those of many other people. There will always be conflicts between unconscious forces. The Self fights for stability.

"You must keep one foot inside the problem, one foot outside it," she said. "Then you can give to the world."

I wondered if perhaps the point where the personal unconscious overlaps the collective unconscious is where the work and the changing go on. Dr. Frey felt that this was so.

Some of my current dreams were now beginning to present me with clues to change:

(169)

I am with a strange, free, healthily irrational woman (like some of the women in Kazantzakis' novels). She is good to be with, earthy, dark, not concerned with what others think. Because of necessity we have to bathe in public in a small enamel bowl. We are naked but it doesn't seem to trouble us. Someone gives me a little black kitten. The woman says it is pregnant. I say it is too young to be. She smiles and shrugs, as if to say that that is how it is.

(170)

A young woman (a patient of mine, very intuitively irrational) has a very tiny baby—hand-sized, a "thumbling"—which she hands to me to care for. I hold the minute infant in my cupped hands to keep it warm. As I look at it, it seems to have become less a baby and more like a moulded lump of clay. I am afraid. I breathe on it to keep it warm but fear it is dying, or becoming less than it was. I wander about carrying and worrying about this strange, clay-like child, who seems now not even to have a face. At last the mother comes, and I show her the baby, and the mother smiles, showing me that it does have a face and a living body and that it is all right.

(171)

I am with a Swiss physician for an examination. Some of it goes on outdoors, some indoors. He puts me on a stationary bicycle to test my heart. He asks about my fantasies and I say that my books tell of those. He checks the lumps and nodules

*of rheumatoid arthritis. Later he says they have discovered cells
in me that indicate a non-malignant but large growth somewhere in me that is taking my energy and must be operated on.
I am discouraged about a new illness. Then a very nice and
competent nurse comes and says a mistake has been made
and there is no growth. There seem to be other patients about,
several of them very irrational or psychotic, and they keep
wanting to touch me or hold my hand in a loving and lonely
way. I have a hard time letting them do this.*

To be with the "authentic woman" of dream (169) was to be
related to that in me which could act lovingly, without pretense,
that which could risk being cleansed without apology. And the
little black kitten showed me once again the dark animal instincts
filled with life. My too-factual side says it can't be so, but the
healthy earthwoman in me says Yes. In (170) came the same
theme of my ego's mistrust in life and the deep trust of the irrational and earthy young mother. It seemed as if my ego could
almost see the transformative nature of the clay, but could not
yet perceive the life force. Dream (171) pointed to the need for
both the masculine dimension evaluation of my inner complex
and for the feminine dimension sense that the complex was there,
but not as bad as it seemed. Certainly my ego needed to love the
irrational, wounded sides.

After this sequence and its meanings there began to emerge a
series of inner dream statements about my urgent inner demand
for higher spiritual consciousness. And to be told that I must bear
the pain of the religious struggle to release others from whatever
I had put on them, and also to be me in the "cloud of unknow-
ing." I realized, too, that I must not at this time run away into
writing, too much doing, helping, thinking—but must stay close
to the small things, with feminine dimension responses, quietness, love, wordlessness.

This demand for higher consciousness meant, of course, going
deep into the unconscious. The central inner dream statements
were these:

(172)
I am in Egypt—but also on the top storage floor of the Vati-

can. I am supposed to be at some other place to meet someone. Two gamin little boys are to be my guides but only if I will go their way, which is finding a route down through the many floors of this enormous building. At first I am impatient with their teasing ways, and then realize that this is the chance of a lifetime—to see this place. First I have to scrape and pull away a pile of debris, bits of burning wood, in order to expose the cover to an opening downward. I lift this and squeeze through to the next level down. From then on we go in a maze from level to level, seeing strange things. In one room weavers—like Egyptians—are working on cloth. At another level I am in a small suite of rooms of lovely soft green colors. Could I stay there? The outstanding scene was of finding, at a deeper level, a remarkable piano. I touched the keys. Then I looked inside and found that the interior hammers are an entire scene, done in delicately carved ivory, of human beings and angelic beings and when a key on the piano is touched a hand, or foot, or wing, of these beings touches the proper string. Each note is clear and right.

(173)
I am with a large assembly of people trying to do a serious seminar on psychological-religious meanings. But many of them are milling about, talking idly, trying to practice pseudo-Zen, etc. Finally I climb onto a wobbly chair and say to them that those who are not serious should leave because the way is costly, it requires hard work and authenticity, and that only in these ways can anyone find Life. Finally we have a small and serious group to work at the seminar.

(174)
I am climbing Mt. Pilatus with many people. It is night. When we stop to rest, a man asks me why we are doing this. I point to the top, where in the deep darkness two lights glow. I say we are climbing because those lights are Joseph and Mary.

(175)
With many people intentionally sinking into a contemplative silence, except for one satyr-like man with a stringed instrument which he plucks as he flirts with women. Then even he grows more quiet. Then we are listening to music and I help them to

begin moving with it. Finally I am standing by a large table
with many brushes and oil painting equipment and a large
painting surface of some kind. A friend comes, and I feel part
of the material is mine and part hers. I say to her that I want
to paint the Cry of Kazantzakis, and ask if she wants to work
with me. She is excited and we begin improvising with color
and form except that I say it should be a great mouth as if the
Cry were being seen from inside. We work together with joy.

(176)
There is a crazy man among us. He is trying to poison himself
and us. I—with the help of others—am trying to watch over
him so he will not do this. We take dangerous things away from
him. We all try to help. He is to be feared but also he is pathetic.

Dreams (172)–(175) described aspects of this particular stage
of the journey. Dream (176) comforted me because it seemed to
say that this negative and fiery masculine destroyer was being
reduced in size, kept in his place. Although I carried such a
demon inside, other members of the inner group were ready to
keep him harmless and pathetic. If he did not exist we would be
perfect—a very dangerous condition indeed.

As Dr. Frey said, it is better to "build small fires" and "spill
a little wine" than to be perfect.

Shortly before leaving Zurich for San Francisco—a little over
two weeks—I had two important transitional dreams:

(177)
The words, "A request for a gift from Tao to complete the
work." The words, "A mother gives a spear to overcome sin."

(178)
I visited the grave of Rainer Maria Rilke, feeling into his atti-
tude toward things, angels, children, and recalling how he
struggled with his own problems by pouring them out into
beauty.

Both of these dreams sharpened my need to find an even deeper
relation to my own creativity by way of writing, and especially
writing poetry again. It serves me as it served Rilke. It is both a
"request" and a "spear," carrying the positive masculine and

positive feminine dimensions in many ways.

To follow the ways chosen for us by the Other, the Omega, the Cry, is to find ourselves, again and again, in unexpected places. As Dr. Jung said, life is always bringing us up against the

> uncertainty of all moral evaluation, the bewildering interplay of good and evil, and the remorseless concatenation of guilt, suffering and redemption. This path to the primordial religious experience is the right one, but how many can recognize it? It is like a still small voice, and it sounds from afar. It is ambiguous, questionable, dark, presaging danger and hazardous adventure: a razor-edged path, to be trodden for God's sake only, without assurance and without sanction. (*The Archetypes and the Collective Unconscious,* p. 217)

The Tao had been requested, but had it arrived? The spear had been delivered by the Mother, but how was it to be used?

I could never have anticipated that the Other would choose for me to be in bed with bronchial pneumonia my final week in Zurich. No walks in the snow, no Christmas shopping, no visits to Maria of Einsiedeln. But this is the razor-edged path. As I look back on it, it was the most helpful thing that could have happened because it forced me to be still and to think about all that had been unfolding during these months. I learned (or tried to learn) penance, patience, how to love and bless what I did have, what a small window's view could give, how very little of what I thought mattered really did, how time is in the last analysis meaningless, and how small a space can constitute a life. I even wondered, lying in bed, if perhaps I might be beginning to learn something of what it meant not to be anxious at the core. Perhaps this illness was to teach me that I belonged to the Cry alone, and that nothing really belonged to me.

This was my first dream when I arrived home in San Francisco, tired, still sick, suffering from jet lag:

(179)
A beautiful feminine voice came from nowhere saying, "Are you home?"

I woke up, reached for my journal and wrote as fast as I could.

Journal

The beautiful voice had the lilt of caring concern. I ponder what it might mean, being led in rich rhythms from the *Song of Songs,* about the voice of the turtledove heard in the land, about the comeliness of the beloved with the dark skin. Something in me knows, although it does not yet understand, that this may be the beginning of the transitus from the dreams of being dispossessed and of choosing to die, to some new movement of the dark night which may lead to a totally different structure of living and being at home. I am afraid. I am also filled with Love that has a mysterious direction.

I am also pushed to write this down in a different way, and I feel that in some way I must push the long anguish and growing into a form, as if this creative overflowing, no matter how self-revelatory or painful, will become one of the ways of religious beauty.

I remember myself in tears in the Chagall chapel in the Zurich Fraumunster when I first saw those exquisite living windows from the soul of the octogenarian artist, hearing the great organ as background for the incredible beauty of a fine contralto voice. I said to myself that I could be a religious artist. I could be. In some way this "homecoming" is part of that.

The feminine dimension kept at me and stayed with me, to my amazement and gratitude. Less than a week before Christmas I dreamed:

(180)
I am with others facing a nativity scene. Everyone begins to sing. I am seated near the scene, and a little girl, about four years old, comes up to me, climbs onto my lap and we begin to sing with the others. Then I see that on my right is a young nun, singing and smiling at me and at the child on my lap.

I wakened with a deep sense of happiness that both nun and foundling child were filled with new joy and we could move into the new year with a very different spirit.

The following year, 1972, was a special year of new growth. Sometimes a year has a particular kind of voice with a particular kind of message: 1972 was like that. It said to me, "Move! Go

downward, deep into the collective unconscious. Work with the
dark earth of alchemy and find treasure there. Find out who you
are. Seek out the dark for its most creative meaning. Move!''

I had twenty-seven dreams having to do with finding my identity. Here's one example.

> (181)
> *I went with a large group of people on a crowded train to
> another city. After being there a short time, I felt estranged and
> wanted to go back where we had come from. I tried to find out
> where to get the train but the horror was that I could not remem-
> ber my name, where I lived, and the purse I was carrying had
> nothing in it that I recognized.*

On the other hand, I had many dreams having to do with a new
sense of meaning and direction.

> (182)
> *In a village with simple people concerned with authentic mean-
> ing and deep inner work. There was a church there of pale
> green marble, where I had often gone with Harry. I knew in the
> dream that it is not what we theorize about or discuss that
> matters, but what we are and do in and with our life that is the
> real meaning of existence.*

And I had fifteen dreams that had black people or blackness in
them. However, the best indicators of what was going on in me
were a series of peak dreams—ones that set forth in the strongest
terms and images the new directions. The overall feeling of them
was that I was exploring a level of the inner world deeper than
any I had previously touched.

> (183)
> *I'm traveling in the country through fields, steep hills, all snow-
> covered. I am with a horse, walking beside him, he on my left.
> There is no sense of riding him. We are together. Equals. Our
> pace is slow, mostly because of me, I feel. He is my friend and
> my comrade.*

> (184)
> *We are traveling, staying the night in an unknown location.
> The surroundings are half wild, with mounds of earth, wild*

plants, etc. At some point a small furry black and white mon-
grel bitch dog comes to us. She is lost or abandoned and is
being harassed by larger dogs. She is friendly and loving, and
I want to keep her. A friend says, "Well, you said you'd have
another dog when one found you. And she has." I pick her up,
feed her table scraps, give her a basket to rest in, chasing a fierce
male dog away, and then try to think of a name.

Dream (183) became intensely important because I began an
active imagination with this great horse, who said that his name
was God's-Earth. He helped me in feeling rooted and secure,
more grounded and willing to move slowly. Dream (184) moved
also into the same active imagination, because the black and
white dog announced that her name was Fuzzy and that she
wanted to travel with God's-Earth and me. These two added a
genuine pagan aspect to my spiritual journey.

(185)
(Wakened with a sense of having gone to depths I had never
touched.) Some friends and I are in a huge city. Most of the time
I am exploring alone. I go through various labyrinthine ways
deep down into the bowels of the city. I go through shops, pas-
sages, roads. I recall one shop filled with beautiful antiques
from many periods of history. Also there were roads where
people walked, and other shops, and schools. The most awesome
thing was that the city was on the sea, and that when I was deep
down into the city it was as if I was under the sea. Once I
could look through a porthole-telescope opening in the city
walls and could see into places where great movements of water
were taking place. Also at one place I saw great waves breaking
over rocks, and boats in the water. And it was as if I went up
to the surface of the city many times, each time by a different
route, and then descended each time to see other parts of this
city. Once I returned by a frightening staircase spiraling up and
up in absolute darkness, but with guides from time to time
telling where to go. On one trip I passed through a room with
a mother animal and her young, and I spoke with them. There
was no fear in the dream, only the electric sense of an unknown
mystery.

This dream let me descend into some archetypal part of my

soul where I needed to be at this time of my life, telling me that I needed to ascend and descend into all the levels of the inner City, in all the ways that I can learn in order to feel more at home there. I needed to see deeper than I ever had into the sea of the unconscious, be born out of darkness, see the fertile instinctual places, protect the still unstable part of me from immersion. It portrayed for me the religious task to which I must be faithful.

(186)
I am in a small coastal village. I wander off alone and come to a small street and odd little antique shops with ancient doors—with green and gold trim like an alchemist's laboratory. I am looking for a bed. I find one in simple wood—and when I see it I realize that I want it and some other simple furniture and a place where I can be alone, introverted, with lots of time to write. Two women, youngish, greet me and say they know me. One reads a tribute to me, the other will honor me by planting seven bean seeds. A farm man and I help her turn soil with sticks we have picked up until deep dark sewage water comes bubbling out to enrich the soil, and I'm up to my knees in this mud but I do not mind.

All the alchemical material I knew rose to the occasion of such a dream. First, after I had written the dream down, I was filled with a sense of being inside my skin in some healing darkness place from which I had felt separated both by work and health. The simple wood, the gold and green colors, and the desire to be alone and introvertedly creative were clear. The two feminine figures startled me. The one who used words was more understandable. But planting seven beans! There are seven eyes of God, seven planets, seven songs, seven metals, seven branches to the Menorah, seven pillars of wisdom, and both the Moon and Saturn move in multiples of seven (28-day or 28-year cycles).

Jung points out that, while seven sometimes seems ominous and produces anxiety, it is also the number of the highest illumination. But what about beans? They are mythically related in many cultures to the dead and the underworld. They are world-wide food, fast-growing and nourishing. Folktales are full of magic beans, and they were related to the spirit of the Food

Mother in Egypt. The stirring of the soil until the rich sewage mixture fertilized it was marvelous alchemy. I realized that the food of my life would not grow until I was willing to go to the lowest places to help it. We were really at work in what Jung calls "the alchemical chaos . . . the *massa confusa* which has contained the divine seeds of life ever since the Creation." (*Psychology and Alchemy,* p. 138)

The same all-inclusiveness and realism of the mystery of Life appeared in other dreams of the dark earth and of seeds and plants that grow from the dark earth. These dreams gave me courage and the sense that much inner and outer changing had taken place. Other dreams told me something like this: You need to live and to fulfill your life as all others do—not as extraordinary or special. Never forget how deep the relationship between you and the inner child must be. Relax in whatever place is flowering, unique, human, struggling, learning, loving.

So, at the end of 1972, much rending and sewing had been done, much extension of boundaries had happened, both in me and in my human relationships. Time had been as often uneasy as easy, but perhaps time had been oftener used creatively than wasted in self-denigration. Life held grace and much joy, as well as many persistent problems which, even so, were now easier to live with.

XIII

Beginning Harvest (1972–October 1976)

Turbulent inner movement and turbulent work at human relationships made these four years important ones. Despite the fact that I work with people much of the time in individual therapy and seminars, I am essentially a solitary and have had few close relationships in my life. But what I have had have been important and lasting. The other side of lasting is hard work! Harry and I put in many hours of turbulence in relating, and the two friends with whom I still share a city house, common work as psychotherapists and seminar leaders, and travel, are friends because of years and years of struggle, fighting, disagreements, unbelievable personality differences, and willingness to change.

My experience is that the more one's creative flow is released, the more suffering and the more joy there are. It is like birth. One is excited about the creation going on inside, one bears it with pain, and one is overjoyed when it comes to pass. These years held a series of such pregnancies and births for me. The paperback edition of *A Magic Dwells* came out, as did two volumes of poetry, *Joseph's Son* and *Braver Than That,* as well as my children's novels, *Knee-Deep in Thunder* and *Hunt Down the Prize.*

The Choicemaker, which I coedited with Elizabeth Howes, also became a paperback, as did *And a Time To Die* (also Howes and Moon)—after its two hardcover editions in England and the United States.

Several magazines had accepted poems of mine. I kept writing full steam most of the time, to my great amazement. One novel, not yet finished, continues to lure me. A second book on Navajo Indian deities—this time focusing on the very feminine dimension of deity—was underway in 1976. Poetry was, during these years and up to the present, my deepest expression. For several of these years I taught college classes in psychology and mythology. Our Guild seminars grew in number almost unbelievably, so that we were having them every weekend and throughout the summer, and had added several weeks in spring.

To be sure, all of this is very outer. Yet at the same time, it happened because something was changing inside, releasing creativity and confidence. It did not happen without deep struggle and inner work.

I went to Zurich again in 1974 and 1976 for continuing work and study. These years also included trips to Malta, Greece, Catalonian Spain, Mesoamerica. There were many returns to loved places in the United States, as well as more time spent at the Guild Center in northern California. Here my cabin became my beloved burrow—where I could paint, carve, write, be.

One of the first problems to present itself for resolution was that of the inner Father. As many of my dreams make clear, beginning with the very first one about hell and the Devil, the negative masculine pursued me from early years. In early 1973:

(187)
My mother is white, my father is black. I do not feel I was a child in the dream, but an adult. For some reason now lost the black father and I were in distressing conflict, upsetting to both of us and to the household. We live together. It is as if he hurt me and I hurt him, yet neither of us wanted to. I am with him (them?) trying to explain how hard it is to be in this situation, how I try to be loving and kind, how deeply I care, but that it is very hard. I go to him, put my arms around him and

hug him. He hugs me just as tightly. I am crying hard. It seems a sad and hopeless state. It is raining outside. My cat gets out into the rain. I say to let him go, because he will have to leave eventually.

At first I felt this as totally negative—but as I pondered it I sensed some vital and long-awaited truth with healing in it if I could face it. The archetypal father was connected with my huge blackness, my negative Saturn, the Pope of Darkness, Satan, the evil men in dreams, the destructive masculine law-and-order dimension. But however and whenever, he was my father here, not my enemy, not demonic, and in the dream we were bound to each other in love despite the almost unbearable friction and tension.

The sense of sadness, loneliness, rain, was how I did feel sometimes, for no outer reason. Here the reason was being stated—conflict between my ego and the dark logos, inevitable conflict, as between the older Titans and the younger Olympians in Greek myth, or between First Man and Woman and Changing Woman in Navajo myth. Yet the two generations of an evolving individual must relate in love, caring, concern, although not denying the problem. My darkness had always been strong, almost overpowering at times, but I had never seen it as a difficult but loving inner parent. Here the childish "I" had to outgrow its hopelessness. Relationship existed here between the I and the dark other. I felt this dream relationship on a new level—one quite different from being ruled by the dark hurts or hostile fathers or from denying them any existence by running away into egocentricity. The tears, the rain, the sadness, the dark embrace—I began to feel these as part of the ego-dissolving process of alchemy, so necessary before real transformation. As Jung wrote; "The philosophers shed tears over the stone . . . so that it loses its blackness and becomes white."

I began to sense that this dream was a description of the new *nigredo* in which the paradoxically tormenting relationship between me and the shadow-father had to be resolved, or dissolved in the alchemical sense, by letting the cat of the lower instinct go into the unconscious rain, and by letting the "I" pour its tears

over the conflict situation so that a bridge could be made across
the imperfect humanness of me struggling for greater wholeness.
During the following year I had twenty-one dreams dealing with
my relationship to black people, black animals, black gypsies,
black children, and black seeds.

Another large area which opened up, sometimes into a flood
tide, was my own writing as a central expression of my Self.
Consciously I was giving more time to it but also the dream voice
began telling me what I needed. For example:

(188)
*I am living in some camp-like place with many women and
children, mostly babies. Babies and toddlers are everywhere.
I go for a long walk through the fields and then beside the sea.
I am served strange food. I write poems. Before returning I
write another poem as a resolution of the first ones. With others,
I said, being very excited about this idea of writing a poem at
the beginning and another at the end of a period of journey,
"It is like distilling alcohol from a large vat. It comes out pure
and clear."*

This dream had a Charles Williams kind of feeling, as if all kinds
of people were cared for under the Omnipotence, as he would
have said. I also had a dream which spoke of creativity in a larger
way, drawing on mythic themes of magical birds which dive to
the bottom of the sea to bring up earth for creation, or climb to
upper worlds to bring magic back:

(189)
*I am going about in various situations and among people,
carrying in my arms a large water bird. It is a wild bird—
like a merganser, loon, or cormorant, but none of these, and
yet it is tame. It is somehow related to children (maybe to help
in a pediatric ward?). I am carrying and caring for it. It is quite
heavy but I enjoy it. Its head sometimes rests on my shoulder
as if I were carrying a child. It gets some excrement on me but
I don't mind at all. And eventually I do put it with children,
perhaps in the hospital ward.*

Creativity must be natural and simple, free-flowing as a bird
would be. In this way, the inner child, wounded but creative, can

be healed. Three other dreams seem to me related to this break-through of my own creativity:

(190)
I spent all night in a huge, underearth world, fantastic but real. There are many small animals and many people, and giants sleeping, and great reliefs on the walls. A woman intro-duces me to some young people who are dedicated to working at this world, saying that we would like each other. I am given a large and beautiful golden dog, like a Chinese temple guard-ian dog. He is fierce, fast, beautiful, and very hard to ride. But I know that I can.

(191)
I am in a huge, strange city-complex. There is a procession of circus animals going on, almost as a religious procession. There are people about, and shops, hotels, etc. I am telling them, or teaching them (the people), a story incorporating the mean-ings of all the things in this city. I am burning with a creative passion to communicate the deepest interpretations, and can-not stop writing and talking, as if the symbols and images kept tumbling over and crowding each other.

(192)
I seemed to spend much of the night telling people of the incred-ible work of the ancient people in America in breeding and raising corn.

(193)
I am talking to a group of young people about the Great Land (as in my novels) and about what is needed to work for the healing of the Great land. Then an older group asks me to tell them about my time with the younger group. I do so, with much humor and excitement. I wakened with words that I had been saying to them

> *Frew and tow*
> *outer and inter*
> *witches in a waterglass*
> *ride on splinters*

(194)
I am with many friends in wild and high mountains, and much activity is going on, especially relative to art. D. B. is

there, being his most loving and most creative self, and we are passionately drawn to each other. There are many ardent moments but always with people near. He is doing small, strange, and lovely marble reliefs and religious figures, and I hope he will give me one. Later on I am working alone at an impressionistic painting, putting white lines on it like circles or stars against a darkish background of sky and cloud. I say I am calling this painting The New Approach.

My conscious mind could not have been as creative as my unconscious Other in choosing the images of creativity which appear in these dreams.

In the long difficult years of growing into a person, of finding the Self/ Other relationship, of trying to understand Meaning, some personal experiences and encounters stand out above others —experiences of love, hate, passion, rejection, acclaim, death, mercy, heaven and hell. Dream experiences also stand forth as ultimate statements of inner quest. As, for example, my early dream of death, hell, and devil. One such dream, or dream series, came in the midst of the previously discussed creativity dreams. I want to tell it and then give my own journal struggle with it at the time, which is better than anything I could add later.

(195)
I am in a big city, driving or walking. I go down a long hill to the ocean, and I see kids sliding downslope in the dirt. One boy in a narrow sled-boat slides right into the sea, which is running high waves. He rides one and won't be able to make the next, I fear, but he does, grounding safely on a piece of earth sticking out of the sea. Someone is with me, watching. A woman friend (?) We see where houses have been smashed by mud slides, and I remark how foolish people are to have built in such places.

Then it seems I have tried to destroy myself by burning myself up in a building or in an automobile. I have been depressed and confused as to where I am going in life. But my try didn't succeed. People know about it, and I am unhappy because I feel now my life and work will be ruined. My friend is trying to help me, trying to get me some work in a clinic or something, but we both know that everything will be against me, and I am sad to be causing her such trouble.

Next, I am walking alone. Perhaps in the same big city (?) A woman comes up to me and greets me, saying she is a children's librarian and likes my books. She is going to a meeting and wishes I could speak but says they have no funds to pay me. I say because I love children and their needs and causes that fees are unimportant. I go with her. She introduces me to the group.

I seem to be in a natural bowl, outdoors, and speak from a high place at the bowl's rim. My words are ex tempore and free, as if I were self-reflecting. What I say is: "I am. Everyone has to start back with an I am. It lies behind everything we are." (Here I wakened, talking aloud. In this half-sleep state I knew that what I was saying in the "I am" speech is the resolution of the suicide attempt. And I fumbled sleepily with ideas for a story, and with the sense that all my writing is a deep part of what I am and of how, like Goethe, I can work out and resolve the dark complexes into a place of peace. I fell asleep again.)

Finally, I dreamed that I am staying in a friend's house, a woman. Now, although it is rainy and stormy, I feel I must find my own home. I go out to do so.

What I wrote then about this dream still holds true:

Journal

I am more aware recently that perhaps dreams of the "city" are more related to Charles Williams' idea of city as perhaps a symbol of the psyche with all its complexes and archetypal connections. I believe that is true in these dreams. I am not here lost in the city, as in many past dreams. It is as if I were going about in it so that I could now assimilate many things.

On the place where conscious and unconscious meet—this downslope to the sea—the healthy boy child (an animus which is neither withdrawn nor arrogant but spontaneous and free) can go into and out of the unconscious without being swamped because he knows there are bits of land even in the sea. I need to know this, to affirm it joyfully. It would diminish my "ghosts."

Once again the child element is underlined. Over and over I am being told how I must find the inner child and be helped by it as I interact with it, see it, heal it, serve it.

The suicide attempt by fire is the most frighteningly real confrontation I have ever had with my intense, negative, self-destructive side. I am a much more moody person than most people know, but here it says I can't stay hidden, that I must see how black it is. I must see that it hurts not only my work and me but also those I love by intruding into their space of life. It hurts me by blunting my creativity, turning me away from joy, sunlight, involvement with passion in life!

This is a genuine resolution. I wakened with a wonderful feeling, while still talking aloud, that I was at a new level of inner creation. This bowl-shaped theater place was like half of a globe of the world, the earth half of the heaven-earth sphere. I was standing at the intersection of the above and the below, saying the words of a new creation—"I am."

The woman who is the children's librarian is the one with whom I stay and then leave for my own place. A loving, warm, inner wisdom, concerned, vital, full of genuine devotion, she nourishes the child, helps me and the Other to say I AM, and lets me go toward my own home. This is a new creation in the making. It is connected to alchemy, in that after an apocalyptic death by fire a new creation comes like a child taken from the tomb of the old and put into the womb of the new.

Such a dream is only valuable as it is enfleshed and lived in the outer world. That is to say, what it tells me as dreamer and journeyer has to do not only with my psyche's movements but with the I AM of the world as well. If inner experiences remain only inner, no matter how exciting they may be they are only a trip in the worst sense of the word.

In the spring of 1974 we went to Malta for the first time, and then to Greece, mainland and islands, to meet the Guild leaders and take them into the Greek world. During this time of renewed wonder and fatiguing joy, several dreams showed me where I was and where I yet needed to be.

(196)
A sense of a long, very intense dream, hard to capture, about being in a situation with many people. One woman especially was central, a serving woman who is half insane. I am with her. I realize that she is possessed by the archetypes. I care for her very much. Later I think we are together somewhere, and

*naked people—a woman, a man, a young boy—are being put
into oven-like places and heated in order to repair their psychic
wounds which show as physical ones. The scene is strange,
frightening, moving. Later I see each of them, and feel deeply
related to them in a new way, and they are healed although
they have scars.*

These words cannot describe what I experienced. Stunned, I
awakened and stayed with the dream a long time, realizing that
there *were* archetypes, that they truly *existed,* that they were part
of God, could be worked at and could bring about changes in
me. It was like a mystical experience of the Other, the many-faced
Other, and I had then a deep sense of faith and of knowing, as
if I would never be the same again. I saw clearly that this is what
I had to do with inner knowledge—let the archetypes act through
me for healing, both of myself and others, to see humanity naked,
scarred, but healable.

(197)
*We (?) have acquired a huge new place for seminars, high in a
wild rocky, Greek countryside. The earth is reddish brown and
the land has steep slopes seaward. Part of our place is still
under construction. Nearby, or as an adjunct to our place, is
an art studio where people are learning. At the entrance is a
small seated statue of a man with an erect penis (similar to
statues of Hermes found at Greek shrines), and a sign saying no
one is to make crude comments about it. There are many people
at the place engaged in self-exploration. At one point I climb
very steep stairs onto a high rock ledge and down again, carrying a small animal and miming a speechless simple child in
order to indicate what the attitude to the journey should be.
Some of those watching me begin to sing folk songs, cradle
songs.*

This was a very different experience of the Other, more concerned with the relationship between logos and eros, stressing
the need for genuine simplicity and earthiness as the work of
becoming proceeds. As I feel into it again, it seems to me one of
the best descriptions I have ever had of religious self-exploration.
The very next night came this:

(198)
*The scene, as much as I can recall, is in mountainous country,
with a very steep-sided chasm-like canyon around and in which
the action takes place. I am the central figure. I have the power
to become invisible, and I am using this power to act out a
drama which can help others to learn what it means to become
"selfless" in the sense of being true to the Self unegocentrically,
and of being loving without demands. Over this canyon are
many ropes on which one can swing, raise or lower oneself,
etc. I become invisible and do this, ascending and descending
great heights in space, swinging in arcs and circles, landing
accurately at certain spots. All this I do with reference to other
people, women and men. I swing out to touch them unexpectedly, or to elude them if they are caught in ego problems. I
ring bells in various places as I move about in space on the
ropes. Sometimes I sing or chant while I am thus moving about
invisibly. At some point there is great positive affect regarding
some feminine person I am teaching. Also there is a great
negative affect regarding some male person whom I am sub-
duing by evading him with my invisibility, keeping near him
but out of reach, chanting over him.*

This dream defined selflessness as an invisible healing power.
Whether in fact I have any such power except toward myself
remains a question. Several psychics have told me that I could
be a sender of healing. This I do not know, but certainly some
power to deal with the inner negative masculine and positive
feminine was manifested to me here.

While we were still in Greece, almost a month before Zurich,
this preparation dream came.

(199)
*Our group seems to have arrived in Switzerland in a moun-
tain village. There is, unexpectedly and extemporaneously, a
gathering of gypsies of all ages for a religious-musical event.
A man I seem to have known somewhere is leading a singing
group, and says that some fine singer is to solo. Then a procession of men, women, children come through the woods carrying
a banner of Joseph. They sing, shout, use fetishes like prayer
sticks. It is both grave and exciting. I am barefoot, watching,*

*listening, following, climbing over and through obstacles. Once
a friend in our group puts a hand on my shoulder and asks
where I am—as if I were transported into some deep inner
place.*

My first experience of the unconscious so long ago was of a
dwarf telling me to listen to gypsy music. A gypsy Joseph, wor-
shipped barefoot and with song, would be at the farthest point
from my negative Pope of Darkness, my Saturnine repressive
side. This dream gave me a good feeling about myself, where I
had come to and where I could go if I worked at it. It had genuine
happiness in it.

This newness was underlined by a further statement:

(200)
*Something about animals, like dolphins, that could be swum
with or flown with in free relationship. I feel that I can do this.*

Finding the ease of movement of a free creature has always been
hard for me. This is related to my feeling function, which does
not have ease of movement—or maybe it does, but only in certain
ways. This "swimming-flying" can come to me from nature, from
hearing music, from hearing children sing or adults laughing or
weeping, from watching a loved person move about, and from
my writing. It is harder for me to bring forth such feelings among
people. Not that I don't have them, but that they have too often
run away into hiding when people demand them, and relationship
is a demand, not necessarily negative but difficult for me.

It is hard for me to swim or fly freely. The bird or dolphin
moves freely in its own element. The bird is land or air, the
dolphin water or air. The dolphin is warm, friendly, intelligent,
joyful—a free spirit. If I could conceive of my feelings as dolphin,
letting them leap from the unconscious into conscious living
and back, in and out, alive and curious, not bound by oughts,
happy, advancing and disappearing as they naturally desired—I
would know a new kind of relaxed joy. This dream was the first
of many that I had of dolphins, and each one has pushed my
introverted feelings further into freedom.

After Malta and Greece, we went to Zurich again. As I review

the inner work I did with Dr. Frey during that period, I see that
the major themes were the usual ones: various ways of making
the Self manifest; the positive role of Jupiter in my horoscope;
the essential need of letting myself go into and stay in prison
(my introverted sources); the negative and positive relationship
to my feelings and how I could make this better; the problem
of the parental poison; the danger of my metallic animus and
how to cope with him; how to accept the nature of my archetypal
introverted feeling; religious sense and feeling needing always
to be, for me, related to the chthonic realm; the need to recognize
how life-giving my creative side is; the acceptance of new and
tentative relationships to the psychic realm.

A few days before we left Zurich, Dr. Frey challenged me:
"Aren't you really more accepting of your own unique reality?"

I had to say yes. I did feel that I was much more at peace with
what I was as a person, that I could bear myself with a little more
ease. I knew then that when I went home I had to have the courage to bear the guilt of my weaknesses and not be angry or distressed when they surfaced. This is the human condition.

Dr. Frey pushed me to acknowledge how deep my introverted
feelings are, how they emerge richly in my creative work. Prob-
bly because I have this creative place it has saved my life. I needed
always to be faithful to the wounds, to my life in its uniqueness.

"Your creative urge," she told me, "is your marriage."

To give a concrete example of what she was talking about, this
dream came during our work together:

(201)
*I find a sad little kitten someone had abandoned. It is dying.
I comfort it. Then, with the help of a friend, I seal it into a living
branch of a tree where it will be transformed, and will have a
new name.*

A small, lonely, hurt, earthy animal part is to be reborn, renamed,
transformed. Such a dream comes straight into that place which
is most sensitive, vulnerable, lonely, soft, easily hurt. This is a
feminine place concerned with evanescence, time passing, all lost
and lonely things. The dream said that I, ego, knew the name

of transformation and must speak it. I must name, in order that it would become. The small loneliness could be made over in the cambium layer of the Life tree.

From 1974 to 1976 my outer professional life grew, seminars at the Guild flourished, and I gave lectures and seminars at graduate schools and other places. Poetry came freely and often, which was a joy. It was a period of rich inner movements and difficult outer changes. Specific dream symbols kept repeating themselves—inner themes with variations, so to speak: illnesses, especially of sight; feminine groups; unusual births; messy or old or crowded or alien residences; underearth and undersea places; wounded children; and dreams of religious rites and symbols.

There was no question but that I was being told that I wasn't yet always seeing clearly into my life:

(202)
I am being fitted for new glasses by an old man who wears glasses with a left lens at least twice as large as the right lens.

(203)
My eyes have an incurable disease where the fluid is leaving them.

(204)
My glasses are smashed.

(205)
A cruel male doctor taunts me because I am mute and blind.

(206)
I am lost, my glasses broken, and I cannot find an optometrist.

As the year went forward, I spent as much time as possible in my beloved cabin at the Guild seminar acreage, in the containedness of my small home there as well as in the beauty of the land surrounding it and the creatures living on that land. All worked together to lead me into new and needed places. I wrote more— particularly poetry—which seemed to be the most satisfying way for me to wrestle with myself and my inner growth.

The saving fact for me, in light of all that was boiling up in me and in my life, was that we planned to return to Zurich in October

1976. Knowing that, I worked as best I could with my uprushing inner voices, spent hours at my painting, worked with seminars and patients adequately, wrote poems, and attended to relationships.

I was deluged with dreams and spent much time with them and in meditation. I walked in the hills with my dog while meditating aloud. (This latter practice seems to interest the birds rather than disturb them.)

Gathering up all this spiritual and psychological burgeoning can, I believe, be best described as filling a barn to overflowing with analytical work, as the next chapter tells.

XIV

Filling a Barn
(October 1976–January 1978)

(207)
*In a large building, part a home and part a place for classes.
I am with a woman resembling my physician. She is beside me
holding my hands, getting me to relax, working with my body.
I realize that I am being prepared to deliver a child. The woman
works to get me to part my legs, relax thighs, etc. Many people
are moving about. Then I am up, wandering somewhere, feeling that I am bumped by the man who may be the father, and
I am trying to find a place alone to bear my pain and my child.*

(208)
*I am in a wide and open place, grayish in impression, build-
ings, yards, fields perhaps. I am pregnant, at the point of
delivery. I am trying to get away from the father, or one I
think may be the father. Somewhere a nurse helps me, takes me
inside, and I have my child.*

(209)
*I am with many people, and we are acting out the sense and
meaning of the Life Force. It is like a cosmic child being born,
with long scenes of effort and travail and strain to show this
Birth.*

From these dreams it was quite obvious that much was coming to birth in the psyche even if the ego was having a very difficult time with it all and kept asking, What is going on here? What is there that needs help? Who is the father? and other questions that at that time had no answers. The closest to an answer was dream (209) with its reference to the cosmic force, the Life Force.

As I looked over these dreams I asked myself: What do I move toward the analytic journey with? What child, what children are to be born? I knew that I longed to further simplify my life, to find what was really basic in order to live more creatively. I knew that I wanted to find my true home, my own life's meaning, my own inner city. I knew that I needed finally to come to terms with what was left of the negative masculine dimensions of impatience, irritability, drivenness, overdoing. How much of this I could understand or even touch in the short period of analysis in Zurich remained to be seen. Nonetheless, it was with relief and joy that I began my time, not because I believe that analysis is the ultimate solution for a life, but because I am absolutely certain that, for me, these periodic workings with a caring other over the long years have given me the necessary mirror to see who I was and how I could be more of that.

Also, the persons I have had the good fortune to work with have all been religiously committed to the life process. None of them has told me what to do, or what I should become, or how I should live my life, or tried to make me more assertive or more attractive or more anything. They have listened to the depths of me and helped me to listen better. They have been, each one, earnest journeyers themselves. All this is by way of saying that to deal with my dreams and responses as I am doing is to present the language of the Self, the music of the inner cosmos.

Just before leaving for Europe I once again laid out the Tarot cards in the same way that Dr. Fierz had laid them out for me long ago in Zurich. The results were once again startling but helpful. To my amazement I had the Maison Dieu in the same place as before. And in places of great import were the Trumps of Pope, Judgment, Death, and Fool. Of all these, the Fool card is most important to me. I have had many fool dreams since then and now have a growing sense that the Fool—not only for me but for many planetary citizens—needs to be related to as the archetype of the twentieth century Savior. Jesus anticipated this when he said that the Son of man has nowhere to lay his head, although the foxes and the birds do. The Fool, for me, has been the toppling of push, thrust, demand, and achievement. The Fool has been the gypsy side, the airborne freedom, the willingness to give over to whatever the weather may be, inside or out, but not to be defeated by it.

In 1976 (and forward) I had many dreams which seemed to me to have in them the element of Fool.

(210)
I seem to have rediscovered, refound, a wonderful and warm and unusual family that I had known at some other time. There were children, parents, aunts, uncles, cousins. They seemed gypsy-like, wanderers, and we have met to journey again together. I wept when I found them, I was so overjoyed to see them once more. There were also with them many animals—tiny squirrels, dogs, horses, snakes, etc. A deep sense of love and trust seemed to pervade the entire odd company. We knew our way had many dangers, but we were together to meet them.

(211)
I am with friends who seem to be harassing me for all sorts of things—attitudes and actions towards my work, my friends, my relationship lacks, etc. Sense of disorder, confusion, mess, conflict, alienation from friends. Then I got into a relationship with a young man, a therapist, living like a tramp on the fringes of the city, no possessions except a blanket or so and a few pots and pans. He is a helper for me, consciously, because he lives this way, almost as a poor mendicant, and helps others. In one scene we are in his hovel, together in an old bed. He curled up against me like a child. "I'm old enough to be your mother," I said. He only smiled. He was composed, relaxed, quiet, and gave me simple food and help from time to time.

(212)
We—mostly women and a few men—are building a fort against an enemy. The enemy, male, may attack from the air,

as well as from the ground, and may use strange and dangerous air machines. We are making our crude fortress of logs and planks. I help where I can, and then I urge the women to disguise themselves by putting on clown costumes.

(213)
I am at some important event, perhaps a wedding, in a semi-primitive outdoor setting. My task is to care for a little girl of three or four years. She and I are in odd clothing. Somehow I know that I do not belong to any class—neither adults nor children—but am sort of a fringe servant (or bridge) related to the larger event.

From these inner tellings the meaning of Fool has begun to take on many more dimensions than I had originally perceived. It has the quality of gypsy, of warmth, of willing acceptance of difficulty, of simplicity, of the child or the "classless servant" of (213), of the journeyer who is also a wanderer (as the Son of man), as that which has identity and yet is never twice the same, of that which is never successful and yet is always successful precisely because it is never successful. Oh, what a lovely, gay parade of items for a person like me who has always been plagued by their opposites!

When I worked on (210), Dr. Frey said that Jung's opinion was that when such a dream of fulfillment came it was as if a new life began, and thus a whole series of new problems and changes in many directions inevitably followed. I learned that this was true. Yet the new problems and changes could be dealt with in ways unknown before my rediscovery of the gypsy family. For instance, I could see more objectively how my wound has been since childhood deep and raw, that my feelings of ugliness and unlikeableness led me to try always to please, to do the helpful thing, to achieve, to succeed, to drive myself, to try to fill the needs of my friends so that I might be more acceptable, and to be hurt again if I wasn't. A dreadful merry-go-round. It seemed as if the various aspects of the Fool were pushing at me precisely so that I could let go of the suicidal ignoring of the substance of my life and could return to my real being—as in some of the dreams given earlier.

Dr. Frey and I plunged deep into the dreams of the past two years and the now. A special dream presented itself to me shortly after my arrival in Zurich. The night before the dream I had attended a moving performance of Schönberg's *Survivor of Warsaw,* a sort of cantata in one of the famous Zurich churches.

(214)
All set in scenes of wilderness, huge mountains, valleys, rivers, forests. My people have been vanquished by a barbarian horde —killed, imprisoned, tortured, held in bondage. But we are slowly planning and carrying out our escape to freedom. Secretly, little by little and under cover, we are getting our people away from hospitals, prisons, and mental hospitals— people of all ages, people filled with fear. We imbue them with courage. We all relate again in love, in passion, no longer afraid. In twos and threes, and in small groups, we struggle against the conquerors. (I was at the same time with my people and of them, and yet also was seeing it happen.) We climb impossible mountains, ride horses across wild rivers, but never as an army, as host against host. It is a struggle of small groups, men and women together, carefully, secretly, against a massive but mindless and unprepared enemy. And now and again, during a respite, there is love-making which leads to renewed courage.

The barbarian enemy has clearly been my fiercely cruel side which wants to imprison, hurt, or render mindless my weaker parts. It has, as the analyst said, always been difficult for me to reveal myself and my feelings. (She referred in this connection to Simone Weil, the French philosopher of religion, as so vulnerable and unprotected that her death was almost an involuntary suicide.) I had had several dreams of bats, which led us to consider the fact that I had a real connection to the dark world of omens, the occult, prophecy, etc., although I had largely ignored it. She questioned whether, just because my consciousness was so vulnerable about feelings, perhaps the depths of the unconscious might be very sensitized in me. I had to agree that this seemed likely.

Dream (214) is one of those dreams that is planetary as well as personal. All of the planet is in, or is fast approaching, this sort of enemy domination. Our mechanization of all things, our assumption that if our weapons are big enough we are safe, our use of fossil fuels as if they would last us forever, our pollution of air, land, and the seas—all these things *are* the "barbarian horde" that will have us in total imprisonment and torment before too many years have passed. Our alternative is, as in the dream, to begin to see individual selves and to relate one to another in love and concern. As Jung wrote:

> In whatever form the opposites appear in the individual, at bottom it is always a matter of a consciousness lost and obstinately stuck in one-sidedness, confronted with the image of instinctive wholeness and freedom. This presents a picture of the anthropoid and archaic man with, on the one hand, his supposedly uninhibited world of instinct and, on the other, his often misunderstood world of spiritual ideas. [He], compensating and correcting one-sidedness, emerges from the dark and shows us how and where we have deviated from the basic pattern and crippled ourselves physically. (*Collected Works,* Vol. 8, par. 190)

Another dream, coming a few months before (214), turned out to be a major event. Among other things, the consideration of its meaning led Dr. Frey to suggest the writing of this book, and led me to take the suggestion seriously but with misgivings.

(215)
I am with friends in a big city. Our entire concern is with rites and ceremonies to be given for Hindu gods and goddesses. Each of us had to be sure that offerings and prayers were given to that deity most related to our particular need. There was much difficulty finding the right place for worship. The most vivid scene was of seeing a woman—perhaps a priestess related to a goddess—wearing almost as armor a great carved screen of beautiful light wood with scenes of the life of Buddha. When I half-wakened in the night I kept saying the name of Kali over and over. And it was there when I wakened. So I felt that Kali (served by this priestess) for me was the one to whom prayers must be given so that healing may come.

I knew little about Kali, and what I did know I did not like.

However, I began to learn more. Kali is often related to Capricorn (my birth sign) as the gate to meaning. She is Saturnian. She is goddess of war, plague, darkness—but also is considered by many Hindu sects as the highest of all forms of Shakti. If one knows her material world fully, one may then reach liberation. Like Capricorn, her light is born in darkness—one must face darkness in order to be reborn. Her terror, horror, desperation, must be passed through, in which case She becomes Mother of Destiny and Meaning. All these things rang true to me. I wrote this comment immediately after recording the dream:

> If these are the things She is Whom I must pray to and be blessed and healed by, then it requires courage and fortitude and a willingness to go deep into the dark places to bring them all at last to light. This involves becoming increasingly disentangled from the things of this world, the *materia* which has dominated my life. This means people, places, things, attitudes, needs, in which I face the negative Great Mother Kali in order that Her Creative Being may be discovered as Mother of Love and of Loving selflessly.

It became clear that I, as woman, had to face Kali's Capricorn Gate and pass through. She stood at the opposite pole from Mrs. Eddy's Christian Science and its denial of matter, substance, and darkness.

The week following the Kali dream, I had another:

(216)
It is as if I am a cell proceeding through the long ages of life—a cell, a sea life (multicellular), a fish, a sea mammal, a land creature, a human being—always struggling to survive, to live, to love and be loved. As if some eye (I) saw all history passing and passing away, struggling to find love, wanting someone to love it (me). (I feel there was some water creature related to me for awhile, but we could not keep each other.) The eye (I) saw the wreckage of history—all cruelties, kindnesses, love, death, a person self-immolated by fire, ruined ships, crumbled and tumbled cities. (In the night half-asleep I wrote, "all passed and passed and no final being, no final being, a sad sea thing cast ashore.") I also wrote, after recording the dream in the morn-

ing, "O God, flowing with the sea-weed in the tidal flats, take
me with you into the sea reaches, where you go let me go with
you into the deep where life is trying—"

I wrote a poem about the Kali dream and about the cell dream.
Later, after Dr. Frey and I had discussed both dreams and both
poems (which can be found in my book *Songs for Wanderers*),
the suggestion that I try to write a chronicle of my long inner
journey was there again. It had never occurred to me that to
share such a living experience was an obligation. But this hardly
believable notion stayed with me—that perhaps my major giving
to others could be this. If I did not get prideful or afraid. Subsequent hours, days, weeks of inner work were filled with insight
far too rich to chronicle in detail. Yet the trends of growth
became clearer. It was time for me to celebrate a new Self birth
at a personal level, as well as to communicate it at an impersonal
level.

One important learning of this period was the coming to terms
with those transcendental, suprapersonal forces in the unconscious that I had previously taken almost entirely as personal,
and thus had felt great fear for my own stability from time to
time. The dream that began this exploration came not too long
before I was to leave Zurich for home.

(217)
Some man has a dangerous metal capsule. Either it contains
poison or it is a time bomb. Several of us are trying to get it
from him—or to lure him away from it—so we can defuse it.
It feels dangerous.

This led me back in time to a dream in which my brother (who
is in fact a gentle, stable person) was frighteningly psychotic,
having no sense of identity. In another dream, a coworker who is
ignored by friends falls from a high ladder and becomes psychic-
ally upset. There were other such dreams.

All these dreams, I began to see, were related to deeper rumblings
of the common earth of humankind, not only to my earth. To be
sure I shared the fate of humankind, but some people (and I seem
to be one) pick up these forces in the same way that animals

sense the coming of an earthquake. This kind of sensing can be terribly frightening or can be dealt with calmly and helpfully. It is deeply related to the problem of good and evil in God and in persons, and to the burdens the human carries to help God's creation.

I had at that time just finished a painting of the tears of God, and also a painting of a capsule made by a student of mine. His capsule had in it mirrors that reflected colors of the central Mayan gods. Remembering this, I could see what might be done with a capsule such as that in dream (217). We can defuse terrors more than we realize if we put the gods inside them. This of course is why it is so helpful to paint or to work in clay to give homes to the gods. This time I realized more fully than ever before that my "hauntings" were tremors from the deep collective layers of the psyche. My bombs, rays, destructive robots, psychoses were, to be sure, partly mine, but even more deeply they were the planetary evils all were having to face.

One three-part dream proved to be another milestone in understanding new ways to deal with my feelings, which still tended to get buried under "good daughter" patterns combined with my own introvertedness. My friends suffered from this because they never knew what I felt, and I suffered from it because I sensed that it was different from what I acted out.

(218)
I am in some mountain place on vacation. My bed, which is unmade as if I had just arisen, has caught fire. I pour water on it and pull up the covers. Going in later, I see it is still smoking, and wonder if I should get help.

Next, someone has died. Many are around paying tribute. Each of us who knew the person is doing some action to recall and make vivid the person.

Next—in a half-waking state I saw these words painted before me,

> *I stand inside (of, the, in?) silence*
> *judging an ancient sorrow*
> *measuring woe*

What came from this was the awareness that going unconscious leads to angers, irritabilities, negative behaviors. I have to watch these smoulders and put them out, not ignore them. Then I must let go and let past things die with love. Only then can I get inside these deep sadnesses and grieve creatively. What actually came out of these dreams and the accompanying insights was the memory of seeing a funeral of one I did not know but felt the shared sorrow.

I had two more dreams before leaving Zurich.

(219)
I am with many people in a great house. A woman has lost all her possessions. Will friends stay faithful to her in her diffi- culties? I am trying to tell her story to many people in order to help her. I call her Spider Woman. I tell them how she has always taken all her goods and divided them among all, and thus she was neither a cheater nor a cheated one.

(220)
Many scenes of the whole economic system collapsing. Then an old woman is being converted to a new spiritual way, while the old man tries to hold on to the old way. Others are there trying to help and to understand. I seem to have the facts and am being asked questions.

Also, some old wise woman has died and I am asked to do a Remembering Ritual. I do this with a small group. We go to the old woman's classroom, from which the man professor has dismissed his class so that we can be there.

Spider Woman is one of the leading deities of the Navajo Indians. She is there at the beginning of creation. She captures part of the sun for light for human beings. She warns people of the dangers of life and of relationship. She had to do with weav- ing, raising corn, giving advice in times of danger. Small but powerful, the grandmother of all living things, she is one of my favorite goddesses.

At the time of dream (219) I had just finished a painting of a large web against a dark background, and on the web, holding to its strands, were a clown, a bat, a lost child, a cat, and a young maiden. It seemed that Spider Woman certainly needed all of my care and attention. She had supported all of my inner parts fully and unselfishly for so long that now she needed me to help her. Only honesty and directness can be used. Unless the ego cooperates with the spinner of destiny, destiny becomes fate. In the words of the dream, destiny is honest, while fate is unfair. It seemed as if the painting anticipated the dream, or perhaps came from the same depths—and the painting was of the web of destiny, my destiny, with its travelers being fool, bat, cat, child, and maiden. To each of these I owed a loyalty and a service, and that service needed to be letting go, giving over all control of my life, being simple and honest and naive as the Fool is.

A much earlier dream of religious rites in which I had water put on my head and was given a cape and had a cat with me was described in my journal as comic-serious. This, it seems to me, is the Fool—the Fool balancing always between death and life, reason and unreason, laughter and tears, witchcraft and holiness, darkness and light, ease and disease. Although important to me for a long time, the Fool now figures strongly in my work with the Self. The errant and struggling ego has had to descend into its hell before it could begin to take up the Self's needs and make a place for the Fool. I am more and more impressed with our psychic time lag. How far in advance of our ego's awarenesses are the wisdoms of our deeper layers! We are told over and over what is, what will be, but we ignore the message until things fall apart.

Another dream touching on the child and fool previsioned what I was coming now to learn more deeply:

(221)
I am on a long boat trip—river, sea, docks. I am in bed, being cared for. I have a great need for rest. A woman is helping me to learn how to do so. It felt so healing to give over, to be in bed, to rest, to be looked after. Always I felt the ship very gently rocking as it moved slowly over the waters. Also all the while we were surrounded and bathed in wonderful mysterious music of the holy spirit.

The music of the holy spirit must be feminine and soaring music, the indwelling music of God the Mother. It was saying to learn to rest in Her womb for healing, although I did not do it until much later. I am only now learning to listen to this music. Probably the intrauterine life of the unborn is much like this at a totally mindless, unconscious level. How splendid it would be to relax consciously sometimes into the heartbeat of the Mother, listening to the spirit's music, going gently.

In these final days of the 1976 inner work, Dr. Frey and I dealt with one dream that had come at Thanksgiving 1974. My unconscious must have known how important it was and saved it till last.

(222)

I am on a huge spit of land several miles across with many people, known and unknown. On all but a small neck this land is surrounded by high pounding seas. The land is vast, strange, with great vistas of water. It is more like an enormous island. There is a sense that I (we) have climbed up steep and difficult ways from under the earth to get to this place. On the perimeters there are some natural (perhaps reef) barriers, and also man-made earth and rock barriers to keep the seas from invading or destroying the island. I am with my closest woman friend some of the time. At some time my father is there. Many, many people of all kinds are around. One scene is of the ex-husband of a client of mine. He is under a bed, drunk, emerges and tries to hide but I find him and rout him out.

I am pointing out to people the vastness and impressiveness of the seas and barriers.

At another time I am with others and we are holding and stroking and being impressed by a bevy of lovely young wild animals—a golden brown ferret, a fox, lion cubs. We are near a pool or a fountain. It felt as if all the world was on this great island, either trying to live in peace, or to flee from difficulties. It was either beautiful or awful, filled with wonder or terror.

At some point I say, to others or to another, "I will not let you go until you bless me."

This was a true Self dream, with all parts and all opposites being there, including life, destruction, loveliness, choices, blessings, and a sense that my psychic life was balanced on a pinpoint of time. Two dreams about the Jungs added light·

(223)
*In a lovely Italian countryside with small towns and hills,
I come to an ancient ruined city and wander in it. I find an
unfinished page about this place, written by Dr. Jung. I lose
it or mislay it before I can tell others, but I do tell them that
Italy, like Greece, although small in size, influenced greatly
the culture of the world.*

(224)
*I am in some European place with Dr. and Mrs. Jung and
others. I seem to go part way on a train with them. I remind
him that he was going to give me an article on synchronicity.
At some point Mrs. Jung helps him off with a heavy back brace.
Then we are at a large outdoor theater where some important
drama was to be performed. The Jungs were going. Somewhere
kittens were playing.*

Dream (223) seemed to say that the ego knows that wisdom
exists, and unique cultural achievements, but the ego does not
yet have a good hold on those facts. Thus there is need to articu-
late, to communicate the uniqueness of a life. Dream (224) under-
lines the fact of synchronicity ever present in my life and the lives
of others. Dr. and Mrs. Jung needed each other but worked consciously in their individual lives to be individuals, independent
and yet related. Mrs. Jung, especially, carved out a genuine sepa-
rateness of selfhood despite being wife, mother, grandmother,
therapist. Thus, symbolically, I need the inner Mrs. Jung to help
care for the more crippled intuitive animus side. I must honor
what I am as Mrs. Jung honored what she was.

I needed to see that all that had been going on for me was
synchronous, timed so that I could choose consciously to be
able to find a life that belonged to me and to the great drama
of life itself, my own opus. In dream (224) I felt that the kittens
were guileless fools and the Jungs the wise fools. My deepest
need, as I prepared to leave Europe, was to be faithful to the
Fool, as well as to Kali, Spider Woman, and the Dance of Life
itself. All would be in the letting go, the giving over, the toppling
of "goodness."

In a final dream, I was to lay greens on the earth for both the

Faerie Queen and the Snake Queen, and to serve them both. The Snake Queen for me was more chthonic and grounded, and the Faerie Queen in the world of the arts, the intuitive outreaches. My ego was to serve both. The opposites cannot be escaped ever.

The questions I wrote to myself at the beginning of this period had been given strange and unexpected answers:

Follow the Fool.

Let go of egocentric desires and plans.

Plan always to face the overturning of events, for this is how it is in the city.

Be open to the occult, the mysterious, the prophetic.

Put out the negative and consuming fires.

Tell your inner journey as a requirement of Life itself.

These answers belong to one person only. Each of us must seek out our own questions and answers, for there is no rule of the unfolding of the self except that it does unfold.

XV

This Is Not the End (1978 and forward)

How could it be the end? How can anything ever be the end until it no longer exists? At this moment I exist more fully than I ever have. In the last few months I have reached a kind of peace of softer breathing, of gentled desires, of quieter sleep, and of a joy of creation richer than ever before.

There is always what May Sarton, the poet and writer, calls "the work of happiness"—a work requiring as much daily practice as any other skilled instrument requires, but intensely worth it if only for those rare moments when the sounds and colors of happiness make you want to cry out for the wonder of it: unexpected gestures of friendship, the joy of a poetry reading when listeners come alive in response, a pair of sharp-shinned hawks in their courtship flight, a new leaf with sunlight through it like the hand of God, an incredible soapweed plant putting out pale green shoots after it has been lying on a table outdoors for eight months.

These are some of the elements of the work of happiness, but there is always that partner of happiness, the work of suffering. It may be the long dying of someone you care about, or your own suffering, a consequence of the facts of the journey itself—that it is forever the same and forever a strange land, that it is lonely and filled with comrades, and that above all the goal of the journey is the journey itself, made on the eternal spiraling tendril of a vine whose roots and whose tip we cannot see.

So this is not the end. But there are some stopping places to share before I move on again. One is this book itself and what it has meant to me to work through it with so much more pain and joy than I could have foretold when I began.

There is also the rich quality of my solitude—which, because I acknowledge it as natural to me now as I never did before, somehow gives me a greater and quieter joy when I am with others.

With my poetry and with my painting, if the inner climate is right I can spend unmeasured time and be rewarded by a sense of birthing. And wonder of wonders, my negative, impatient, irritable, self-denigrating masculine dimensions are failing in health and losing their strength. This is a beneficence beyond belief to my entire household, inner and outer.

Like an aging tree, I thus provide more shade for smaller growth, more places for nests, and can withstand harder storms.

What is the inner Other telling me now?

(225)
Amid scenes of many people and problems to solve, I see a large, impressive, beautiful (as a rare work of art would be) and stately insect of exquisite pale green. It is alive, and its head with the large insect eyes is surrounded by small insects who are either serving it or (perhaps and) getting wisdom from it. It is like some strange Buddha figure carved from pale jade, yet very much alive.

This dream insect reminds me of the mantids, and of my character the Mantid (in *Knee-Deep in Thunder*) which was also very much a Wisdom figure. What kind of wisdom?—that which resides in the psyche as miraculously as the brain resides in the skull with billions of interconnections available at any moment.

Our inner wisdom perhaps can be like this if we attend to it with the same singleness of purpose an insect seems to have.

(226)
I am living and moving about in a strange landscape with many other travelers. There are animals, people, lovers hand in hand, walking beside winding rivers and roads. There is a Hill of Remembering, a Hill of Forgetting, a Place of Dreams. Throughout I have a tiny thumbling baby to care for. I cradle it in my hands, wrap it to keep it warm, find food for it. It is very active and wiggly. When it sleeps it is like a tiny furry cocoon.

This is the place to which all parts of me can come for healing and restoration—like the healing center of Lavidia in Greece with its waters of remembering and waters of forgetting, where people came to be treated, attended to dreams, and felt reborn like infants.

How astonishing the unconscious is. I did not remember Lavidia when I dreamed this nor when I wrote about it. A friend to whom I told the dream reminded me of Lavidia—whose enchantment was resting quietly in some deep layer of me waiting to be used when needed. At the deepest level of meaning for a life, this is to say that each time there is a new step of growth, there must be certain things to forget and certain things to remember—i.e., forgetting the irritations and unkindnesses of others, and remembering what love really means.

There must also be dreams to work with and understand. Then our thumbling Self (the "smaller than small" and "greater than great") must be our concern.

(227)
I am with friends in a wooded and wild country. A huge felled tree is being pulled through the dark forest, as if the land was being restored and renewed. I had a deep sense of ME—separate from my friends but not alienated—as being on this earth first, primary, having the first claim. My hair is long as a primitive woman might wear it.

This dream came as the fifth one about working with the land, waters, trees, reestablishing my place, deepening and widening and making more secure my boundaries.

Of course there are always those days and weeks and dreams that do not affirm or herald newnesses, but instead tell me that I have in fact slid backward—days when nothing I did or wrote came out creatively, person to person situations felt like disassembled jigsaw puzzles, dreams held up to my sight wounded parts to be worked with, large groups of rebellious and difficult people to be taken in hand.

I have found that there are periods when a particular symbol will repeat itself as a theme with variations. The underearth world has presented itself to me over a dozen times the past year.

(228)
I am living in an underearth (as of the Celtic Faerie, or the Germanic Kobold) and am one of the strange people there. We are each unique and separate but we help one another and can laugh despite difficulties.

(229)
In a great deep chasm, with others, working at the task of emergence so we could come and go on the earth.

These dreams, and others with the same or similar settings, are reminders of several things: creation—for the Navajo myths have all creation beginning underground; my own central relationship to the archetypal depths; and the experienced fact that all emergent newness comes upward.

Six special dream experiences seem appropriate to lead toward the non-end of this telling. Each seems to say its own unique thing regarding present and future.

(230)
With a group of people, mostly coworkers, on a difficult overland journey through wide lands, difficult terrain, great spaces. We were talking of a great American writer and patriot related to war—Hart Crane. And we were also involved in that war's aftermath. Scenes of refugees, us with them, returning, trying to find our way home. There was mingled sadness and gratitude, confusion, fatigue, excitement.

Hart Crane was a unique American poet, writing of the America he saw at that time, caught between machines and the earth, city and land, music and alcohol. He loved the poets Walt Whitman, Herman Melville, Emily Dickinson. The sea was his great symbol, and he wrote of sea voyages and great bridges. He also wrote a poem to Charlie Chaplin as the guileless fool. He was a tragic suicide at thirty-three.

In all these ways he loved the people and the subjects that I love—journeys, fools, the sea, and the American poets. My darkest side, too, was similar to his, and I too have been involved in a war between inner opposites for the last years. Now it is ended at one level, at least, and it is time to find the way home—for the time being.

(231)
I am in a school where one is taught medicine for healing. It is large, labyrinthine, mostly waterways. Students and teachers are all women. We students are practicing with dummies, life-sized, walking or swimming with them through the waterways in vast rooms and corridors. My teachers are two aged women. (Both very dear friends and both dead for many years.) Also it seems I am an experienced student so I am helper to younger ones. I did not always know, but I felt able and glad to help their learning.

(232)
I'm with men and women, learning ways to get in touch with greater Powers. We are using intense concentration, meditation and prayer to achieve a better focus and to use energy in new ways. I am a newcomer and learner, and experienced people are teaching me.

Both dreams say that my ego has much yet to learn of depth and inwardness. Also there is the ego's role of helper (to outer and inner beings) if it lets itself be helped. I was deeply stirred to have as mentors my friend the surgeon who had operated on me, and my friend the artist and professor of art who taught me painting. This combination of earth, water, labyrinth, feminine (as it came in (231)) is the essence of the Great Goddess of transformation and rebirth. (See Erich Neumann, *The Great Mother,*

for marvelous descriptions.) The dream described many of Her
manifestations and said to me, "Go to Her mentors, learn, practice, learn. Here is the Kettle of Transformation." Life, death,
rebirth, transformation—this spiral has no end, just as the spiral
of disorder, healing, disorder, healing has no end.

Three other important dreams more or less previsioned the
central attitudes I need as I move into time future. They are not
final statements but necessary signposts.

(233)
Two other women and I are making our way across a wild,
harsh country. We are in long robes, like pilgrims. There are
large rough roads of lapis lazuli scattered here and there, some
carved. We are trying to solve the mystery of the people of this
land, especially their religion. Most particularly there is a man
to be sought for. He dresses in lapis lazuli. There was fear,
struggle, and fatigue.

Lapis, the Self of alchemy, is also Mercury as a cross of sun
and moon. It is Boehme's "Christ." It makes a quaternity with
the feminine trinity in this dream. Also, the man in lapis lazuli is
substance/spirit; to seek him is the lonely, difficult pilgrim's
way. No other can do this for me. It is never easy to take this
journey.

(234)
I am with Dr. Jung in his home. He is a wise and very old man.
He is sometimes in bed, sometimes not. The dream had to do
with me learning from him and his actions about various
aspects of being human, talking with him about his darkness
and light. I discuss him with a woman servant, she describes
his humanity. Once I see him chuckling about some social
blunder—probably his own.

Dr. Jung accepted his humanness, his unbalances, his wounds,
betrayals, all the false accusations about him. With honesty, anger,
impatience, humor, he symbolizes an inner wisdom figure that
tells me, with a grin, that wholeness does not equal perfection,
that the City of God has both dark and light in it, and that the
ego must stay ever in touch with the human condition.

All that remained of a long important dream were these words scrawled in the night in this arrangement.

(235)
>*Simplicity*
>*purity of line*
>*lean-ness*
>>*for my soul*
>>*for my life*
>>*for my being*
>>*for any being*

Simplicity, purity of line, lean-ness—these are not finality words, period words. They do not describe mechanical things but refer to things in motion, in creation, things being born, changing, dying, being reborn. They are words to describe paintings, poetry, sculpture, music, the dance—and sometimes (rarely) lives.

Can I reach some approximation of this condition in my life, my soul, my being? Help others to try? Because this is not the end, I cannot know. I do know that the religious significance of my existence lies in my working for simplicity, purity of line, lean-ness. To the degree that I can learn how to do this in myself I can give something to the planet on which I live.

More than seventy years have passed since the blizzardy Christmas that launched me. I believe I have solved some of the questions put to me then. I am sure there are ancestral ghosts still haunting me, but who of us can say what help we may have given others just by staying on the Journey?

I'm glad this is not the Journey's end, that in truth there can be no end.

SIGO PRESS

SIGO PRESS is a publishing firm specializing in Jungian-related works with an appreciation for its content and its audience.

OTHER BOOKS AVAILABLE

PUER AETERNUS   Marie-Louise von Franz

A study of the positive and negative qualities of the *Puer Aeternus*, the eternal youth and creative child within us. This book includes an in depth interpretation of Saint Exupery's *The Little Prince*. ". . . (Puer Aeternus) is the one book . . . relevant to any effort at making sense of this problem." DAVID HELLERSTEIN, ESQUIRE October 1983. $10.95pa $17.95cl

DREAMBODY   Arnold Mindell

This revealing book ties together theory with case material and traces the *dreambody* in mythology, shamanism, yoga and meditation, ". . . a ground breaking book . . . one of the first to root therapeutic body work in its ancient and rich soil of cultural conscious . . . eminently useful to anyone seeking to integrate their own body and psyche." CHOICE $11.95pa $17.95cl

SANDPLAY   Dora M. Kalff

Dora Kalff's pioneering book on sandplay shows how this dynamic therapy can heal the wounded psyche and result in the successful growth and development of the personality. An excellent tool for anyone working with or interested in art therapy, play therapy and early childhood development.
                                                    Color & B/Wht photos. $11.50pa

IMAGES OF THE SELF   Estelle L. Weinrib

Jungian analyst and Sandplay therapist, Estelle Weinrib, brings new development and insight to the basic sandplay approach and shows how it is successful with adults as well as with children.   Color & B/Wht photos. $11.95pa $15.95cl

DEATH OF A WOMAN   Jane Hollister Wheelwright

This record of a young woman's analysis during the last few months of her life documents the transformation of her experience of dying from one of fear and pain into a process of fulfilment, completion and readiness.
"This is a beautiful account of one woman's struggle and an analyst's courage."
ELIZABETH KUBLER-ROSS, M.D. $12.95cl

LIGHT FROM THE DARKNESS   Paintings by Peter Birkhäuser
                                          Commentaries by Marie-Louise von Franz

A beautiful collection by the mystical Swiss painter. Guided by intuition, Birkhäuser delves into the darkness and reveals images from the collective unconscious.
                        Bilingual, English-German   Color & B/Wht photos $21.50cl

ENCOUNTERS WITH THE SOUL   Barbara Hannah

Active Imagination is thought to be the most powerful tool in Jungian psychology for achieving wholeness. *Encounters With the Soul* illustrates step by step this important method of reaching the unconscious. $9.50pa $15.00cl

SIGO PRESS

S I G O PRESS

77 Washington Street North, 201
Boston, Massachusetts 02114
(617) 523-2321

NAME			
ADDRESS			
CITY	STATE	ZIP	

DATE

QUAN	DESCRIPTION	LIST PRICE	AMOUNT

	SUBTOTAL	
	SALES TAX	
	SHIPPING & HANDLING	
	TOTAL	

Domestic Shipping and handling costs:
Add $1.50 for the first book and .25 for each
additional book sent to the same address.
California and Massachusetts residents add Sales Tax.

All books shipped via Book Post unless otherwise specified. Books will be shipped upon receipt of payment. Sorry, no COD.

Bookstores and wholesalers are allowed trade discounts. Credit applications and discount schedule available upon request.